LOGIC

LOGIC

The Art of Inference and Predication

DENNIS C. KANE, O.P.

SHEED AND WARD: NEW YORK

© *Sheed and Ward, 1969*

Library of Congress Catalog Card Number 68–26041

Manufactured in the United States of America

Dedicated to my parents and my sisters and brothers from whose lives I continue to learn many lessons in the logic of love.

Preface

To multiply textbooks in any field of learning needlessly would be contrary to the "law of parsimony." Each newly published book in logic, then, needs an intrinsic reason for its being. This book is no exception. Actually, it is a fact that it grew out of *three* feelings that I had experienced in studying and teaching logic for ten years: (1) a definite *dissatisfaction* with the pedagogical methods and scholarly tones of most traditionally oriented textbooks for undergraduate students; (2) a frank *disenchantment* with the alleged openness and ideological neutrality of most nontraditionally oriented textbooks for undergraduate students; and (3) that there was a manifest *disrespect* for each other's views that is still prevalent between these two major schools of logicians. In such conditions undergraduate students are inevitably the unsuspecting victims. From such feelings about textbooks on logic was spawned the strong desire to write a book principally, but not exclusively, for undergraduates that would to some extent help to ameliorate these situations. Aristotle advised that in such projects "one must be content to state some points better than one's predecessors, and others no worse." (*Metaphysics XIII*)

This textbook will have an obvious traditional orientation, yet it will neither neglect nor belittle the fundamental notions that have played an important role in the genuine development of nontraditional logic in recent years. By structuring it along the lines of "predication" and "inference," it is hoped that the coherence and unity that is possible and desirable in logical reasoning will be quite evident to the student or the casual reader. Convinced by my own classroom experiences that "horizontal enrichment" offers many challenges and advantages to undergraduates, and aware that suggested trips to the library are not seldom ignored by collegians, I have designedly put a few "pertinent quotations" from experts at the end of almost every chapter. In addition, all the "exercises" at the end of each chapter should be helpful, for they are parts of examinations that were given by me or my colleagues over a period of fifteen years.

Finally, I would like to express my sincere thanks to many people for their contributions to making this book a reality: to my religious superiors, Frs. L. Every, K. Sullivan, and J. R. Gardner for their paternal concern about this project; to my colleagues, Frs. W. Duprey, B. Perz, and P. Kenny for their fraternal help in trying out in their classes the manuscript in its early stages; to Fr. E. Hogan and the members of his library staff at Providence College for their many assists in that area; and to many others for their helpful suggestions aimed at making the text more readable, especially Paul G. Zomberg of the English Department at Providence College. A special word of thanks is due the various groups of collegians and seminarians both in America and in East Africa whose reactions alerted me to the need of such a text. Finally, for a hard job that was done excellently and painstakingly, I want to express my sincerest personal gratitude to my competent typist, Mrs. Patricia D'Ambrosio.

Contents

LOGIC

Introduction

I

To be called *illogical* at any time is a kind of academic censure. Most adults know how embarrassing it is to have a faux pas in their reasoning pointed out to them. Yet, on the other hand, we would feel complimented if, on almost any occasion, someone said to us, "Your argument is quite *logical.*" The logical person is simply one who is wont to engage in discourse in a manner that is both reasonable and fair. Aristotle, the recognized founder of Logic, considered those only to be educated persons who would be able consistently to form a fair off-hand judgment as to the goodness or badness of any activity in the domain of discourse.[1]

However, to be capable of such criticism habitually and with finesse calls for some training in logic. Such an orientation would prove to be advantageous, for by it one becomes acquainted with the guidelines of inferential reasoning that logically-valid arguments and proofs must follow. Applying these recognized norms of validity will then become more challenging and more meaningful. The need of guesswork in such circumstances would be eliminated too. In short, most people agree that in contemporary life the noticeable lack of familiarity with logic is a crippling handicap in the ever expanding sphere of verbal communications.

A brief look at the process of *inferential reasoning* will show the relevance and importance of logic as an academic discipline. Inferential reasoning is a step-by-step movement in knowing

3

something more completely. It comes as easily and as naturally to man as does his tendency to know things in an empirical manner: e.g., through the experiences of seeing and hearing. Such perceptual thoughts afford the data for acts of inference. Actually, inferential reasoning consists in a kind of *drawing out* of a conclusion or statement from a designed combination of two or more previously enunciated statements which are mutually relevant: e.g., (If) every astronaut of the U.S.A. is courageous; (and if) John Glenn is an astronaut of the U.S.A.; then (it follows that) John Glenn is courageous. This last statement is called an *inference* or an *illation*.

To the degree that one is acquainted with the approved laws of logic, one has a greater chance of success in both creative and critical thinking. If formulated correctly, inferences and proofs are said to be logically valid: if formulated incorrectly, inferences and proofs are said to be logically invalid. To be able to make inferences, which is the same thing as being able to *think conceptually*, is an ability that differentiates men from all other corporeal creatures.[2] Logic enables one to make correct inferences more efficiently and more easily.

Still, in no way is this *apologia* meant to suggest that a formal course in Logic is absolutely necessary for the intellectual fulfillment of every educated adult. That would be both an unrealistic and an immature claim. After all it is undeniably true that many logical and compelling arguments have been fashioned by people who never were exposed to any kind of a formal course in logic. But it is also not less true that a course in logic is necessary for the cognitive and cultural *well-being* of all adults. Such an academic subject is necessary at least to the extent that genuinely educated men should be so conditioned as to be able constantly and confidently to distinguish valid arguments from invalid ones, regardless of the area of learning in which they appear: e.g., chemistry, theology, sociology. Besides, there is no other course in the college curriculum (or high school) that has a primary purpose so basic to the learning process. It also must be pointed out that despite the close affinities logic has with both psychology and literature, neither of them is an adequate substitute; nor can any number of courses that are purely mathematical in character take the place of logic in the universe of discourse.

Logic has always been an ambivalent discipline. In its historical evolution, its nature both as an art and as a science has been emphasized. Though the primacy of logic as an *art* has been duly recognized for twenty-five centuries, its stature as a *science* should be neither ignored nor minimized. Since George Boole (1815–1864) this scientific character of logic has received due emphasis in the academic world. Viewed as a science, logic is an organized body of knowledge made up of principles, laws, and axioms fundamental to correct and critical reasoning. However, it is an historical fact that the practical values of logic have tended to outstrip its speculative potential, both as an art and as a science. This is understandable enough, for thinking is seldom an end in itself for most men; they are more inclined to be creative.

Logic has not only been accepted as an *art* over the centuries, but has been awarded a certain primacy. Insofar as logic deals with the products and operations of human reason itself, it has not without merit been called the *art of arts.* To be rightfully considered an art, servile or liberal, a process or activity is measured by the dimensions of its participation in the movement known as ratiocination, i.e., by the extent to which it shares in human reasoning or conceptual thinking. Logic deals primarily, directly and indirectly, with what are technically called *second intentions*: e.g., concepts, words, definitions, and propositions from which arguments are subsequently constructed.[3] Traditionally, since the ancient Greeks, logic has been considered a kind of *second nature* for men, like the arts of dancing and fencing, to the extent that it can help us carrying on our natural operations of inferring with orderliness, poise, and a minimal margin of error.[4] It is also truly a *cooperative* art. Like the medical arts, which tend to work together with the processes of health in animals, this art of critical reasoning perfects man in such a way that his constant pursuit of truth can be both a rewarding and a delightful experience. Logic also affords social advantages because it is "part of the courtesy of conversation, attaching to the virtues of friendliness and pleasantness, which are bound up with truthfulness; for without ease, modesty, and exactness men cannot dwell together."[5]

II

Dissatisfaction with others' arguments and proofs is not an exclusively modern social phenomenon. History tells us that each age, including our own, has had its burning issues which men have naturally discussed and debated. These issues are both national and international in scope; seldom are they purely academic or trivial in nature. Actually, this state of dissatisfaction with arguments and proofs in any sphere of social intercourse can be a signal clearly indicating a healthy intellectual condition, a sign that people are alert to the fact that not all arguments are of the same logical value.

To err in argumentation is as common an event in daily life as it is human. Reasons for incorrect argumentation are myriad. False conclusions can be arrived at even in "good faith." Many arguments are the bad fruit of ignorance or prejudice. Fallacious argumentation takes many forms. Not a few arguments that are logically counterfeit are intentionally so; some result only from excessive emotional factors.[6]

From our disenchantment with others' arguments, even some of those proposed by savants in their special fields of erudition, arises the important question: HOW can we best distinguish valid arguments from counterfeit ones? In other words, what are the neutral, reasonable canons or norms that, like a Geiger is to metals, can be used confidently to test the overall value of arguments? Surely, it can be argued, if gold bullion and diamonds can be so certainly tested, then any argument should likewise be testable: either it will be found to conform to or satisfy a set of objective standards for logical discourse, or it can be rejected as inadequate. Arguments can be defective on two major scores, their *veracity* and their *validity*. Logic is principally solicitous about the latter feature, but cannot ignore the former feature if the perfection of the whole argument is to be evaluated.

(a)

The veracity or truth-value of any argument is related to and rooted in its *content-matter* as represented by the terms of its statements. This view of truth is unanimously held by the logicians of the Traditional school, which traces its lineage back to Aristotle. In this view, only those statements or propositions merit the label *true* if they mirror some conformity between one's conscious knowledge of some reality (e.g., a gaseous substance) and that reality itself in its existential state of being: e.g., some gases are poisonous.

But this is not the only view of truth or veracity. Some logicians, such as A. Tarski, seem to be closer to the traditional view than they realize when they assert that a sentence is veracious insofar as it is satisfied by all the objects it represents.[7] However, truth is commonly viewed by those of the Non-Traditional school of logic as a logical value that can be arbitrarily assigned to a propositional statement by some kind of extrinsic denomination, like a tag on a valise. Their position is understandable enough in the light of the tremendous influence of Humean empiricism, Nominalism, and pure Mathematicism on this school of logic. Operationally, this view of veracity in relation to propositions has many advantages, as will be shown in a later chapter. In the chapter on propositions, some of its weaknesses also will be analyzed.

(b)

Nevertheless, regardless of his view of truth, the logician's primary concern in argumentation is *validity*. But, here again we meet another problem about basics. It is no secret that amongst logicians there is a serious disagreement about the exact meaning of validity in argumentation. This difference of opinion in an area in logic arises from philosophical positions that are radically opposed. In a later chapter the nub of this problem, i.e., the precise nature of the illative act, will be duly considered. At this point we shall simply identify validity, as does the Non-

Traditional school, with the structural exactness or an approved shape or an elegant form in which an argument is cast. Such a common acceptance of the term *validity* will be useful until later on in the book. However, for the Traditional school, validity has a more rigorous connotation. It means that an argument will have integrity in its logical formulation only to the extent that it adequately measures up to the strict requirements of correct inferential reasoning. Mere mechanical juxtaposition of truth-value statements is not enough in this view of validity. These views are not as superficially different as they may first appear; both views are poles apart because they are concerned with the very essence of formal argumentation.

A few examples of arguments, alleged to be *valid*, will help to illustrate this essential element of argumentation to which any worthwhile course in logic should address itself:

(a) Aristotle, *Prior Analytics I*, chap. 4:

(If) all B is A; (and if) all C is B; then, all C is A.

(b) Pierre Teilhard de Chardin, *The Divine Milieu*, Harper Torchbooks (New York: Harper & Row, 1965), p. 56:

> At the heart of our universe each soul exists for God in our Lord; but, all reality, even material reality around each one of us, exists for our souls; hence, all sensible reality around each one of us exists, through our souls, for God in our Lord.

(c) from the writings of Sextus Empiricus as recorded in Benson Mates, *Stoic Logic* (Berkeley: University of California Press, 1961), p. 62:

> If a god has told you that this man will be rich, he will be rich; this god (Zeus) has told you that this man will be rich. Therefore, this man will be rich.

By comparison, the following arguments are known with certainty to be *invalid* argument-forms:

(d) Aristotle, *Prior Analytics I*, chap. 5:

> (If) no N is M; (and if) some O is not M; (then) some O is not N.

(e) Mates, *ibid.*, p. 83:

> If it is day, then it is light; it is not day; therefore, it is not light.

(f) Aristotle, *ibid.*, chap. 4:

> (If) some B is not A; (and if) all C is B; (then) some C is not A.

The degree of perfection in any argument, then, depends necessarily and simultaneously on the presence of these two factors: *veracity* (of content-matter) and *validity* (of form). Both are as essential to the nature of a worthwhile argument as are the proper amounts of hydrogen and oxygen in the molecular structure of water. Any argument lacking in some way, either in truth or in validity, is to that extent an imperfect one. Just as high-speed aircraft, in order to withstand the tremendous demands in stress and strain to which they will be subjected, must be constructed from high-quality durable materials and in accordance with the best-known principles and laws of aerodynamics, so too, perfect arguments must be fashioned according to the inexorable demands of objective truth and logical validity.

Perhaps by now the importance of the *validity* aspect of argumentation is sufficiently clear. Since no respectable logician pretends seriously to be omniscient, the *veracity* aspect of any argument, outside the subject-matter of logic itself, is only indirectly and secondarily his concern. In short, logic is primarily *formal* in character and in interest. Practically speaking, therefore, regardless of the content-matter of an argument (e.g., politics, sociology, biochemistry, metallurgy, theology), the person with some orientation in logic will be well equipped both to discover the logical structure of any informally proposed argument and to arrive at a fair and knowledgeable judgment about its logical value.[8]

Pertinent Quotations about the nature and scope of logic:

(a)

As Aristotle says in the beginning of the *Metaphysics*, the human race lives by art and reason. The Philosopher here touches upon a certain property of man by which he differentiates him from other animals, for other animals are moved to their acts by a natural instinct, while man is directed in his activities by the judgment of his reason. The various arts, then, serve to bring human acts to their fulfillment in an easy and orderly manner. In fact, *art* is nothing else than the certain ordination of reason by which human actions through determinate means arrive at their proper end.

Now human reason can direct not only the acts of the lower powers of man, but also is even directive of the acts of reason itself. To be capable of *reflection* on itself is a distinctive quality of the intellective part of man, insofar as the human intellect understands itself by being able to think and judge its own actions. Hence, just as man is inclined to reason about the artifacts made manually in an easy and orderly manner (e.g., the art of building), so it is necessary for man the artificer to possess an *art* that directs the very act of reason by which in the very act of ratiocinating he may proceed with ease, yet in an orderly and unerring way. *This art is logic*, i.e., rational science. It is *rational* not only because of its harmony with reason, since this is peculiar to all the arts, but also because it is concerned with the very act of *reasoning* itself as its proper matter. Consequently, it is the *art of arts*, insofar as it directs us in the act of reasoning from which all the arts proceed in some way.

> —St. Thomas Aquinas, *Commentary on the Posterior Analytics I*, Preface (Leonine edit.), lesson 1, Nos. 1 & 2 (author's translation).

(b)

And it will not be possible *to be* and *not to be* the same thing, except in virtue of an ambiguity, just as if one whom we call "man," others were to call "not-man"; but the point in question is not this, whether the same thing can at the same time be and not be a man in name, *but whether it can in fact*. Now if "man" and "not-man" mean nothing different, obviously "not being a man" will mean nothing different from "being a man"; so that "being a man" will be "not being a man"; for they will be *one*. For being one means this, i.e., being related as "raiment" and "dress" are, if their definition is one. And if "being a man" and "being a not-man" are to be one, they must mean one thing. But it was shown earlier that they mean different things. Therefore, if it is true to say of anything that it is a man, it must be a two-footed animal (for this was what man meant previously); and if this is necessary, it is impossible that the same thing should not at that time be a two-footed animal; for this is what "being necessary" means, i.e., that it is impossible for the thing not to be. It is, then, impossible that it should be *at the same time true* to say the same thing is a man and is not a man. The same account holds good with regard to "not being a man," for "being a man" and "being a not-man" mean different things, since even "being white" and "being a man" are different; for the former terms are much more opposed, so that they must *a fortiori* mean different things.

> —*The Basic Works of Aristotle*, tr. R. McKeon (New York: Random House, 1941), "Metaphysics IV," chap. 4, Nos. 1006–07; by permission of the Clarendon Press, Oxford.

(c)

The *aim of proof* is, in fact, not merely to place the truth of a proposition beyond all doubt, but also to afford us insight into the dependence of truths upon one another. After we have convinced ourselves that a boulder is immovable, by trying unsuccessfully to move it, there remains the further question, what is it that supports it so securely? The further we pursue these enquiries, the fewer become the *primitive truths* to which we reduce everything; and this simplification is in itself a goal worth pursuing. But there may even be justification for a further hope: if, by examining the simplest cases, we can bring to light what mankind has there done by instinct, and can extract from such procedures what is *universally valid* in them, may we not thus arrive at general methods for forming concepts and establishing principles which will be applicable also in more complicated cases?

> —Gottlob Frege, *The Foundations of Arithmetic*, tr. J. L. Austin (New York: Harpers, 1960), p. 2.

(d)

Hence it must be asserted that *speculative sciences* are concerned about those subjects whose knowledge is sought for its own sake. This is evident in the early part of the *Metaphysics* (3). However, *logic* is concerned with those subjects which are not sought to be known for their own sake, but rather as a kind of help (*adminiculum*) to the other sciences. And so logic is not contained as a kind of principal part under speculative philosophy, but is a special way back to speculative philosophy insofar as it offers to speculation its own tools, namely definitions and syllogisms, etc., of which speculative sciences are usually in need. Whence, according to Boethius in his *Commentary on Porphyry* (4), logic is not so much a science as it is an *instrument of science*.

> —St. Thomas Aquinas, *Commentary on the Book of Boethius Concerning the Trinity*, Quest. 5, Arts: 1 & 2 (author's translation of the Quebec edit.).

(e)

For the philosopher, as an analyst, is not directly concerned with the physical properties of things. He is *concerned only* with the way in which we speak about them. In other words, the propositions of philosophy are not factual, but *linguistic in character*, that is they do not describe the behaviour of physical, or even mental, objects; they express definitions or the formal consequences of definitions. Accordingly, we may say that philosophy is a department of logic. For we shall see that the characteristic mark of a purely logical enquiry is that it is concerned with the formal consequences of our definitions and not with questions of empirical fact.

—Alfred G. Ayer, *Languages, Truth and Logic* (New York: Dover Publications, Inc., 1952), p. 57.

(f)

In our consideration of the *theory of consequences* we approach that field in which we discover some of the finest achievements of scholastic logic. It is in the logic of consequences that the scholastics have reached a high degree of *formality*, which, in the Aristotelian tradition at least, connotes a high degree of perfection. However, we cannot ascribe complete originality in these matters to scholastic logicians, although we can credit them with the discovery, or perhaps the rediscovery of many theorems which hold places of honour even in modern logic.

—Philotheus Boehner, O.F.M., *Medieval Logic* (Chicago: University of Chicago Press, 1952), p. 52.

Exercise:

(1) If a "principle" is "that from which something proceeds in any manner whatsoever," state what you think might be basic principles of arguing.

(2) State what you consider to be two basic principles of mathematics, and of being.

(3) Give two examples of statements that you and your friends consider to be "veracious."

(4) Give two examples of statements that you and your parents consider to be false.

(5) Why do you and your friends or parents consider statements to be true or false?

(6) Is every valid argument veracious? Explain your reply.

(7) Is every veracious proof or argument valid? Explain your reply.

(8) Who is generally reputed to be the "father of logic"?

(9) Is logic primarily a "science" or an "art"? Explain your view.

(10) On what grounds could a liberal arts college omit logic from its core curriculum?

(11) On the assumption that men and brutes are only accidentally different, would man need a course in *logic?* Explain.

(12) How does logic differ from (a) grammar and (b) mathematics?

(13) How is it similar to each?

1

Words and Predication

Communication is necessary for man's well-being in this world. Yet it is an undeniable fact of human experience that successful communication is impossible without the use of some kind of symbols or signifiers. Regardless of their origin or structure, signs or signifiers are indispensable realities for all beings capable in any way of knowledge and self-expression (e.g., a trapped hyena's groans or a barber pole or a saddened bride's tears).

However, not all signifiers in this world are *natural*; some are *artificial*. We human beings recognize early in life that we can use both types of signs for greater self-expression in almost any situation. Psychologists are in almost unanimous agreement that, as uniquely human artifacts, languages arise naturally from an innate social yearning of men to communicate more completely and efficiently with each other. According to some, this universal proclivity is rooted in man's rational nature and accounts in no minor way for the existence of thousands of languages in the world today.[1]

Because languages are instruments that men devise ingenuously in order to translate their feelings, thoughts, and judgments to each other, this chapter will have a two-fold purpose: (1) to clarify the somewhat hidden features common to all signifiers as exhibited by certain, familiar natural signs; (2) to show that the terms employed in all statements or predications are not natural signs, but means of signification which are artificial (e.g., verbal signifiers such as words in ordinary discourse and non-verbal signifiers employed in such formulas as $E = mc^2$).

I

One of the most important features of a sign is its own individual *existentiality*, i.e., every signifier is a reality, a something apart from any knowing agent. Too often this rather obvious feature of a sign is taken too much for granted. Ominous storm clouds, as airplane passengers who have flown through them know empirically, are *real things*. So are those crimsoned skies at the end of day as they presage fine weather on the morrow. No one can deny that the picturesque changing of leaves that harbinger autumn is a real phenomenon in itself.

Besides possessing this independent existence, many things have within themselves a factor of *knowability*, i.e., a capacity to be psychologically grasped. This feature is easily exemplified by the frown on a person's face. Significantly it ordinarily reveals something about that person's feelings, just as a smile usually manifests opposite feelings. Nothing could signify without being grounded somehow in its potentiality to be known. In the Aristotelian-Thomistic synthesis, this feature of *cognoscibility* is nothing other than an intrinsic capacity of an entity to be assimilated in a non-physical manner, either by itself or another knower. This capacity, of course, varies with the objective perfections of the knowable thing itself, i.e., a dog has more to be known about it than a dandelion.

Signs or signifiers, then, are *meaningful* because of their relation to beings that are capable of knowing. This feature of every sign is seen very easily in our common sensate or perceptual experiences. Unless the groanings of an animal, either trapped or in travail, are actually heard by someone else, they will be neither recognized nor appreciated. We know early in life that such phenomena are not only spontaneous releases from suffering but also significant sounds of pain. From our own psychological experiences we know, too, that to a person without the power of sight, a rainbow would be a meaningless symbol since he could not see it. Similarly we are aware that the presence of caproic odors, indicating the existential presence of goats in the area, would not be in any way significant to one whose olfactory powers were inadequate or inoperative. In short, sense images are natural signifiers necessary, psychologically, for any communication on the sensate level.

The ability to communicate in the animal world has many more limitations than in the human world because men are such superior knowers. They have a distinctive manner of knowing. By nature, men are not restricted in their knowing to sensate images or constructs, a mode of communication that is mostly physical in character and closely associated with organisms. This fact we know from our own personal experiences. Strangely enough, however, the human cognitive process has not a little in common with the way infrahuman beings know. It also has much in common with the angelic mode of knowing and communicating, for angels usually communicate with each other in a purely ideational way because of their totally immaterial nature.[2] In other words, their non-physical concepts or ideas are the sole means for their mutual enlightenment. Such ideas are also natural signs to the extent that there is a quasi-intrinsic and causal relation between the signifier itself and whatever is being known or communicated.

Man, then, has a distinctive mode of knowing and communicating because he is a kind of microcosm, a substantial blending of somatic and spiritual elements. Because of this unique nature, man is capable of thoughts that are both perceptual and conceptual.[3] He is the only member of the animal world that can and does employ both types of natural signs, sense images and suprasensate images (ideas). Historically, this complexity of nature has been the font of many of the problems raised by epistemologists.[4] But it has also been the source from which he has been able to fashion a new mode of communication, that in which words would play so important a part. Words are most properly called *signs* or *signifiers*. But, like icons, they are not natural signs, as any English-speaking traveler quickly discovers in Mexico or Pakistan or Czechoslovakia or any place where the native language is not English. Only knowers, then, are able to perceive, interpret and appreciate signs; and the mode of recognizing and receiving signifiers is determined simply by the cognitive perfections with which one is endowed.

Besides their intimate relation to knowledge, every signifier has the characteristic of *otherness* about it. No genuine sign will lack this factor. Noiselessly and unostensibly, all signs must have this tendency to self-effacement. In short, no sign exists for the sake of itself. The ability to *represent* something other than itself is a role assumed spontaneously by signs in the drama of communication, as it is by the diplomats representing their countries' needs and principles in an international assembly. All signs, then, are *intermediaries* between a thing signified and a subject that is capable of knowing that thing. This vicarious role is inherent essentially in every sign worthy of that label.

Regardless of the theory of knowledge they espouse (e.g., Humean, Kantian, Thomistic), logicians are commonly agreed that an entity is a signifier or a sign if and only if it satisfies the *three* conditions we have discussed. Aristotelian-Thomistic logicians have traditionally incorporated them in the classical definition of *sign:* (*1*) *that which represents* (*2*) *something other than itself* (*3*) *to a knowing power.*

II

Predication is simply the meaningful arrangement of terms in a statement. Structured by men for purposes of efficient communication, statements can take the form of equations, formulas, and prosaic assertions. To predicate well is truly an art that enables one to assert something about something else in a clear and meaningful manner. Logic and literature are united in this sphere of education.

For this intended enlightenment of others the most common means employed in the universe of discourse is speech, i.e., words that are syntactically structured for communication. Words or verbal signs obtain their literal meaning from some degree of formal agreement by either the speakers of a language or some authoritative group, like the French Academy or the Science academies. Since some group approval is to some extent responsible for the structure and significance of such terms, words are said to be *conventional* signs. As products of human ingenuity and creativity, words are artificial things. As conventional signifiers, words always have a certain amount of arbitrariness about them. Their structure and significance are subject to the decisions of the group. Non-verbal signifiers, such as those icons used traditionally to indicate bars and barber shops as well as national flags, are likewise subject to changes in their signification. This is understandable enough for there is nothing in the nature of the letters from which the words "dog" and "god" are composed, for example, to account adequately for their polarized meanings.

Despite the ease with which man can create these artifacts of communication, they do pose a very serious built-in problem as far as *intelligibility* is concerned. From experience most of us are aware that unless we are acquainted with the meaning of a conventional signifier, such as the scale of a barometer or a thermometer, it will fail to function for us precisely as a sign. In the concrete, this means that if we do not know the conventions of the Greek language, the verbal sign αγγελος (messenger) will be devoid of meaning for us; likewise, to a non-scientist, the non-verbal signifier, $E = mc^2$, has little or no significance. Not unlike statues or portraits of distinguished national heroes (e.g., Joan of Arc among the French and Abe Lincoln among the Americans), these artifacts to the extent that they are signs have to be known first as objects before what they represent can be understood. In short, languages are not at all as natural and as global in their meaningfulness, as are sunsets and smiles and rainbows. Still, language is the most commonly used method of communication among men.

It may be well to observe here that historically the use of *letters* as symbols in predication is a practice that dates back to ancient times. The use of such non-verbal signifiers is not uncommon in the writings of the Peripatetic and the Stoics.[5] Letters and other simple symbols have also played a substantial part in the remarkable new developments in the fields of logic and mathematics that have taken place since the mid-nineteenth century. However, the use of non-verbal signs in predication is (and always has been more or less) restricted almost entirely to technical spheres where exactness and efficiency are of primary concern. In chemistry, for example, the molecular structure of sodium and some other element is sharply expressed in terms such as NaCl (table salt). In this way it is possible to eliminate vagueness and ambiguity, undesirable features in any kind of scientific predication. Sometimes, these non-verbal symbols are called *ideographic* signs; whereas verbal symbols (words) are often referred to as *phonographic* signs.

Nevertheless, communication by means of letter-symbols especially, being essentially non-verbal, has found little use outside technical areas. Words are much more flexible instruments in meaningful human intercourse. As a matter of fact, ordinary conversations would be impossible without words. As terms employed to translate the myriad aspects of human thoughts and emotions, words have many dimensions of structure and signification. They can be urbane or rustic, simple or highly sophisticated, crude or refined, virtuous or vulgar, colorful or color-less, musical or modish. Still, it is a fact that words are often found, despite their versatility, to be impotent means of expressing our deeply personal joys and sorrows. Yet their excellence in predication is a credit to human genius. Anyone attempting to appraise the relative perfections of a language would certainly have to take into account both the degree of its intelligibility and the subtlety of signification of which it is capable; but this mixed question is more the concern of semantics than logic.[6]

In logic, then, words or verbal signifiers are looked upon as those basic principles out of which all ordinary discourse is composed. Logicians are chiefly interested in those completely meaningful predications or statements which are in some way endowed with a truth-value, i.e., which are either true or false (e.g., some women are not ladies; no Arab is rich). This enunciative type of statement (as opposed to the interrogative and imperative types) is known in the field of logic as a *proposition*, and propositional statements will be the subject-matter of many chapters in this book. By way of summary, then, words are genuine signs because they are man-made artifacts to which a conventionally-sanctioned meaning is attached in order to serve the cause of knowledge and communication in society. In the next chapter, this mode of predication known currently as propositional-language, a phenomenon peculiar to the human race alone, will be subjected to further logical analysis.

Pertinent Quotations about words and predication:

(a)

Any sign is that which represents to a cognitive power something other than itself, as its vicegerent.

—John of Saint Thomas, *Cursus Phil., Logica*, part I, ch. 2; (author's translation).

(b)

Despite the great wealth of our languages, the thinker often finds himself at a loss for the expression which exactly fits his concept, and for want of which he is unable to be really intelligible to others or even to himself. To coin new words is to advance a claim to legislation in language that seldom succeeds; and before we have recourse to this desperate expedient it is advisable to look about in a dead and learned language, to see whether the concept and its appropriate expression are not already there provided. Even if the old-time usage of a *term* should have become somewhat uncertain through the carelessness of those who introduced it, it is always better to hold fast to the *meaning* which distinctively belongs to it (even though it remain doubtful whether it was originally used in precisely this sense) than to defeat our purpose by making ourselves unintelligible.

For this reason, if there be only a single word the established meaning of which exactly agrees with a certain concept, then, since it is of

great importance that this concept be distinguished from related concepts, it is advisable to economize in the use of the word and not to
employ it, merely for the sake of variety, as a synonym for some other
expression, but carefully to keep to its own proper meaning. Otherwise
it may easily happen that the expression ceasing to engage the attention in one specific sense, and being lost in the multitude of other
words of very different meaning, the thought also is lost which it
alone could have preserved.

Plato made use of the expression *idea* in such a way as quite
evidently to have meant by it something which not only can never be
borrowed from the senses but far surpasses even the concepts of
understanding (with which Aristotle occupied himself), inasmuch as
in experience nothing is ever to be met with that is coincident with it.
For Plato *ideas* are archetypes of the things themselves, and not, in
the manner of the categories, merely keys to possible experiences.

> —Immanuel Kant, *Critique of Pure
> Reason*, tr. of unabridged edit. N. K.
> Smith (New York: St. Martin's Press,
> 1965), pp. 309–10.

(c)

Men who have in their hands the future of peoples and of coexistence
among nations are meeting, are holding discussions. Once more the
word *peace* seems to be at the center of their thoughts. Oh, how
ambiguous and fragile and difficult *this sacred word* has become,
although it should characterize human and civil relations among
nations. Yet we must keep this *word* in our hearts and proclaim it, in
hopes that real resolutions for reconciliation, pardon and goodness
will give it *meaning* and coherence.

> —*The Pope Speaks*, Vol. 12, No. 3, 1967
> (Washington, D.C.: tr. document No.
> 3566 appearing in *L'Osservatore Romano*,
> June 19, 1967).

(d)

A sentence is a significant portion of speech, some parts of which
have an independent *meaning*, that is to say, as an utterance, though

not as the expression of any positive judgment. Let me explain. The word *human* has meaning, but does not constitute a proposition, either positive or negative. It is only when other words are added that the whole will form an affirmation or denial. But if we separate one syllable of the word *human* from the other, it has *no meaning*: similarly in the word *mouse*, the part *ouse* has no meaning in itself, but is merely a sound. In composite words, indeed, the parts contribute to the meaning of the whole; yet, as has been pointed out, they have not an independent meaning.

Every sentence has *meaning*, not as being the natural means by which a physical faculty is realized, but as we have said, *by convention*. Yet every sentence is not a proposition; only such are *propositions* as have in them either truth or falsity. Thus a prayer is a sentence, but is neither true nor false.

Let us therefore dismiss all other types of sentences but the proposition, for this last concerns our present inquiry, whereas the investigation of the others belongs rather to the study of rhetoric or of poetry.

—Aristotle, *ibid.*, "On Interpretation" or "Hermeneia," ch. 4.

(e)

If man used only sensate knowledge, which pertains to the here and now, the significant utterance "vox" would suffice for him as for the rest of animals insofar as through special utterances they manifest to each other their own sentiments.

If indeed man were naturally a kind of maverick, his own soul's passions would be sufficient for him as an end in themselves; but, because man is by nature both a political and social animal, it was necessary that the ideas of one man should be made known through utterances to another man; therefore, it was exigent that meaningful utterances "voces significativas" come into existence so that men could *socialize* easily. Whence, those who are of different languages, are not able to do this very well.

An utterance is something natural, whereas a *noun* and a *verb* signify from human institution. This comes to something natural, like matter, in the way a bed is formed out of wood; in order to designate the makeup of nouns and verbs, Aristotle says *those things which are in utterance,* as if it were being said about a bed, *those things which are in wood.*

A *word* (oratio) is meaningful not merely because of some natural capacity as an instrument. The natural faculties of the *interpretative capacity* are the throat and in the lungs, by which an utterance is shaped; literate and articulate sounds are fashioned differently by the use of the tongue, teeth, and lips. Besides, a *word* and its parts are as *effects* of the interpretative capacity by means of the aforesaid instruments. As a motive power uses natural faculties, like arms and hands, to fashion *artifacts,* in a similar way the interpretative capacity makes use of the throat and other natural instruments in the fashioning of a *word.* Therefore, a *word* and its parts are not so much natural things as they are *artificial effects.* And so *a word signifies by convention "ad placitum,"* that is, according to the institution of human reason and will . . . just as all artificial things are derived from the same source.

> —St. Thomas Aquinas, *Commentary on the Hermeneia of Aristotle,* lect. 1, 2, & 6 (author's translation).

(f)

This also is asserted to be most evident, that it is proper to man to use speech through which one man can totally express his idea to others. Indeed, some animals mutually express their feelings in common, as a dog is wont to show anger by barking and as other animals manifest other feelings in different ways. And so man is more *communicative* than any other animal.

> —St. Thomas Aquinas, *De regimine principum,* lect. 1, cl. No. 1 (author's translation).

(g)

Logicians, so far as I know, have done very little towards explaining the nature of the relation called *meaning,* nor are they to blame in this, since the problem is essentially one for psychology. But before we tackle the question of the meaning of a word, there is one important observation to be made as to what a word *is.*

If we confine ourselves to spoken words in one language, a word is a class of closely similar noises produced by breath combined with movements of the throat and tongue and lips. This is not a *definition* of "words," since some noises are meaningless, and meaning is part of the definition of *words*. It is important, however, to realize at the outset that what we call one word is not a single entity, but a class of entities: there are instances of the word *dog* just as there are instances of dogs. And when we hear a noise, we may be doubtful whether it is the word *dog* badly pronounced or not: the noises that are instances of a word shade off into other noises by continuing gradations, just as dogs themselves may shade off into wolves according to the evolutionary hypothesis. And, of course, exactly the same remarks apply to written words.

It is obvious to begin with that, if we take some such word as *Socrates* or *dog*, the meaning of the word consists in some relation to an object or set of objects. The first question to be asked is: Can the relation called *meaning* be a direct relation between the word as a physical occurrence and the object itself, or must the relation pass through a *mental* intermediary, which could be called the *idea* of the object?

—Bertrand Russell, *Logic and Knowledge: Essays 1901–1950*, ed. Robert Charles Marsh (New York: The Macmillan Co., 1956), p. 290.

Exercise:

Classify the following signs as NATURAL or CONVENTIONAL:

(1) . . . . a fever as a sign of illness.

(2) . . . . thunder as a sign of an impending storm.

(3) . . . . footprints as a sign of living being in the area.

(4) . . . . a recording of 90 degrees on a Fahrenheit thermometer signifying hot weather.

(5) . . . . frost on the ground in autumn as a sign of cold weather.

(6) . . . . the word *sayonara* in Japanese as a sign of farewell.

(7) . . . . the number 8 signifying a specific quantity.

(8) . . . . the sense image of some object existing in an animal.

(9) . . . . a rosy complexion on a child's face as a sign of health.

(10) . . . . pulsation in a man's arm as a sign of life.

(11) . . . . the word *logos* in Greek signifying *word* or *study*.

(12) . . . . the idea of *justice* as it exists in the minds of political leaders throughout the world.

(13) . . . . o degrees Centigrade as a sign recording freezing conditions.

(14) . . . . a frown as a sign of some kind of irritation.

(15) . . . . the American flag with its stars and stripes signifying the democratic way of living.

(16) . . . . a clock as a sign of time.

(17) . . . . the concept of flower as a sign of some kind of plant.

(18) . . . . gold as a sign of wealth.

(19) . . . . the word *jambo* in Swahili signifying welcome in Africa.

(20) . . . . a kilo signifying a measure of weight amounting to 2 lbs. 2 oz.

(21) . . . . the molecular structure of H_2O as a sign of water.

(22) . . . . a sunset as a sign of the end of the day.

(23) . . . . a red-colored traffic light signaling to stop.

(24) . . . . the word *equus* in Latin signifying a horse.

(25) . . . . the concept of *empathy* as it exists in the minds of most people.

2
Concepts and Predication

If language makes predication possible, and if exact predication is such an important factor in the sphere of human communication, then it is feasible that an analysis of the fonts or sources of predication be made. That is the main objective of this chapter. Common sense seems to indicate that, unless words or verbal signifiers have some relation of dependence upon concepts (ideas), *words* in any language would be meaningless artifacts and communication would remain at the level of infantile babbling. But, since present-day communication is in such a highly developed state, we can validly infer that there is some necessary alliance between predication, knowledge, and objective reality. In short, it is demonstrated to us in our everyday experiences that the *way one knows* an object influences the *way one talks or writes* about that object.

I

Aristotle gave us simple guidelines to guarantee meaningful discourse when he wrote that "to say of what is that it is not, or of what is not that it is, is *false*; while to say of what is that it is, and of what is not that it is not, is *true*."[1] Since concepts are natural signs in the suprasensate level of human knowledge, they should mirror objective reality; otherwise there would be no reason for their existence. Yet, to deny that each of us possesses ideas would be contrary to our own personal experiences.

Concepts are, then, *intermediaries*. They are intermediaries between the *words*, into which all meaningful statements are resolvable, and the *objects* as they exist individually and from which all human knowledge naturally originates. Only when so grounded in being does predication reflect reality and serve *truth*.

Words or verbal signifiers are called *predicates* when they are employed in statements enunciating that an attribute belongs or does not belong to any *subject*. Like the things they signify or represent, *predicates* sometimes refer to one thing or class, and at other times to many things or classes: e.g., omniscience as attributed to God, and speed to cheetahs, and knowledge to men and animals. However, despite the great diversity of possible predicates there are only TWO general or supreme categories to which they all can be reduced: (1) *essential*; (2) *non-essential*. Predicates are said to be *essential* or *substantial* if and only if they signify attributes or traits necessarily connected with the nature of the thing, like the ability of toolmaking in relation to man. Such predicates can be employed in *four* different ways. Predicates are said to be *non-essential* or *accidental* whenever they signify attributes which *may* either belong or not belong to any one and the self-same thing; a man may at one time be standing and at another time be lying down. Yet he is the same man regardless.[2] Such predicates can be employed in *nine* different ways. Each of these two supreme modes of predication, traditionally called *predicables*, will now be analyzed.

II

That which principally characterizes all the predicates correctly classified as *essential* or *substantial* is that they have some intimate reference to the very core of a thing. In other words, this kind of predication is necessary because some entities do exist as *substances*: e.g., oxygen, cats, giraffes. These predicates are known as *genus, specific differential, species, property*.

(1) A *genus* is a predicate that can be said of a plurality of entities whose natures have much in common, yet have profound differences. To a question about the constitution of such an object, such as What is it?, this type of predicate would be a correct but an incomplete reply: e.g., All men are *animals*; All roses are *flowers*. The number of subjects in statements to which this type of predicate can be attributed is very *extensive* because in its scope even opposites are included: e.g., the notion of *habit* is as common to vices as it is to virtues.

(2) A *specific differential* is a predicate that can be said of a plurality of entities which are not the same numerical individuals or the same in kind. Such a predicate signifies a radical principle that makes one kind of thing to be unlike another kind of thing, even though both would be in the same general class or group: e.g., sodium and silver; cows and horses and elephants. The earlier logicians were wont to use the example of the constitution of Man, whose animality is contracted and determined in some intrinsic way by the element of *rationality* which is reflected in his capacity to think conceptually: e.g., All men are rational; Some animals are not rational. Experience teaches us that the specific differential factor of most things is difficult to discover. Nevertheless, scientists in every field of knowledge must face up to this constant challenge. Logicians have recognized the need to clarify further the notion of this important predicate for their own uses as well as those of the other sciences.

(3) A *species* is a predicate that can be said of a plurality of entities that share a nature or an essence *in absolutely the same way*; i.e., they are the *same kind* of entity: e.g., All his pets are *horses*; All skiers are *humans*. To the question about the "within" or reality of an entity, What is it?, this type of predicate should be a reply that signifies a thing's *entire essence*. The excellence of a thing's definition, as will be seen in the next chapter, is determined by the accuracy with which the *exact species* (*infima*

species) of an entity can be discovered and expressed. Experience in classifying things will show also that the number of subjects to which such a specific predicate can be rightfully attributed will then vary inversely: e.g., animals-horses; flowers-roses. As a predicable, *species* is actually nothing more or less than the substantial fusion which involves a thing's generic features and its specific differential. Hence, there are species of birds (robins —bluejays), fish (trout—dolphins), color (blue—red), motions (up—down), qualities (angularity—virture—vice).

(4) A *property* is a predicate that can be said of a thing's essence insofar as it belongs (1) exclusively, (2) always, (3) necessarily, and (4) to everyone of its kind. Yet it does not enter into the essential composition of the thing itself, i.e., it is not a part of its essence. Still, it is an attribute that is predicated convertibly of the essence.[3] Man is a good example for he alone, according to psychologists, can be credited with such properties as the ability to fashion and follow rules of syntactical speech, the ability to make tools and icons, and the ability to be humorous and witty.[4] Taken in its strictest sense, a predicate is attributed to a subject as its *property* if and only if the four conditions are satisfied simultaneously:[5] e.g., All men are capable of laughter; All corporeal entities are subject to gravity. Still, there is a generally accepted tendency to employ this type of predicate in a less strict manner in most sciences. However, it is a sign of an educated person to be cognizant of the manner in which he uses this predicate in his own statements, as well as how others use it in their statements. Carelessness in this regard has not seldom been the source of many ambiguous assertions in the sciences.[6]

III

All other predicates are properly labeled *non-essential* or *accidental*. In this supreme category are contained all those predicates which signify those many attributes which may or may not happen to a thing, i.e., attributes which are neither essential parts of a thing nor a thing's genuine property. That there are many more accidents than substances in our world is self-evident. Understandably, therefore, accidental predication is the most generally used in human discourse. Yet, it is evident that without singular, individual substances (*this* cow, *that* man), modifications and movements, i.e., accidents, do not exist in the real world:[7] e.g., redness in a sunset; knowledge in an animal. In other words, because dogs and snakes are *real entities*, so also are their sizes, colorings, and movements. Every accident indigenously tends to inhere in or adhere to an individual substance. An *accident*, then, is that predicate which expresses a changeable *condition* that can be present in or be absent from an individual thing or a plurality of things, yet without any interference in their substantial or necessary constitution: e.g., Some men are *pale*; Not all women are *five feet tall*; *Helen is sick*; Some horses are *faster than others*.

An *accident* can be employed as a predicate in *nine* general ways. Two of these ways—known as *quantity* and *quality*—express an absolute adherence of an attribute in a subject insofar as these attributes tend to be totally independent of anything extrinsic by which they are so denominated. The other seven ways of accidental predication have this in common that they do not tend to express this absolute adherence in a subject itself, but have an element of *otherness* about them. The differences in these two major modes of accidental predication will become clearer during our analysis. These seven ways of predicating accidentally are known as: *action, passion, relation, time, place, posture,* and *dress*.

(a) The accident of *quantity* is a predicate that can be said of a substance that is material in its composition insofar as it is disposed to have a *mutual ordering of its parts*. Aristotle holds that quantity is essentially divided into *discrete*, as exemplified in numbers and speech, and *continuous*, as exemplified in lines and surfaces and solids.[8] The following statements illustrate this predicate:

The Berlin wall is *ten feet high.*

Some elephants *weigh two tons.*

Not all numbers are *unequal.*

(b) The accident of *quality* is a predicate that, when attributed to a substance, causes it to be said to be such and such: e.g., scientific, or virtuous, or a good boxer, or sweet and sour, or hot and cold, or curved and triangular. It is evident that the term "quality" has myriad meanings. As a predicate, it can be extended to all those *attributes intrinsically modifying living and non-living things*: e.g., *habits*, such as contracts that are just and thinking that is mathematical; *dispositions* of mind and body which are *easily changeable*, such as diseased, ignorant, scrupulous, healthy; *potencies and impotencies* naturally inclining one to do something rather easily or to avoid painful things, such as being a clever thief, an honest person or an illiterate one; *affective qualities*, insofar as entities that possess them are so described because of them, as sweetness is to honey, blushing is to shame, and turning pale is to fright. Aristotle observes that there is still another kind of quality which consists of the *figure* and *form* of things, such as rectangular, circular, or elegantly shaped as applied to artifacts like statues and buildings. The following statements illustrate this predicate:

The Masked Marvel was a *good wrestler.*

Some pyramids in Egypt are *triangular.*

Not all soldiers are *courageous.*

All wine is not *sour.*

(c) The accident of *action* is a predicate that can be said of the subject that does something to something else: e.g., a hunter *shoots at* a target, a carpenter *strikes* a nail. The scope of this predicate extends only to *transient* actions, not to *immanent* ones. Immanent actions belong more properly to the predicate of quality: e.g., smelling, judging, thinking. The following statements illustrate this predicate:

> Jim Londberg is *throwing*.
>
> The men are *painting* the house.
>
> The hoodlums are *beating* the hippies.

(d) The accident of *passion* is a predicate that can be said of a subject which in some way from without is being changed or being acted upon: e.g., teeth being *extracted*, a bridge being *bombed*. Whenever the term "emotional" is used in predication to signify the normal movements of the irascible and concupiscible appetites, it is properly a predicate of quality: e.g., Blanche is *angry*; Irving is *hopeful*. The following statements illustrate the predicate of passion:

> In World War II London was frequently *bombed*.
>
> The police car was *struck broadside* by the truck.
>
> Laurette had never been *kissed*.

(e) The accident of *relation* is a predicate that can be said of the *order* that does or can exist between things in any way whatsoever: e.g., something is *greater than* something else; something is *less beautiful than* something else. In most relationships three features are present: the *basis* of the reference, its *other term*, and the *subject* which is referred (e.g., the birth of a child is the basis for the relationships of paternity and filiation). Other examples are the relationships of slave-master, student-teacher, husband-wife, employer-employee, coach-players. Aristotle insists that this predicate in any kind of meaningful statement always signifies some form of reciprocity between things. The following statements illustrate this predicate:

> The Taj Mahal is *more beautiful than* the White House.
>
> Miss Mitchell is *his teacher*.
>
> Not all American beers are *inferior to* Heineken's.

(f) The accident of *time* is a predicate that can be said of a subject insofar as it is measured or measurable by the earth's movement around the sun and its rotation on its own axis: e.g., this *morning*, last *year*, before *dusk*. This predicate indicates WHEN something is to happen or has happened. The following statements illustrate this predicate:

> The Superbowl game took place *in January.*
>
> The Israel-Arab war lasted *one week.*
>
> The Vietnam war has gone on *for five years.*

(g) The accident of *place* is a predicate that can be said of a subject insofar as it is, if materially constituted, surrounded by its first and immediate surface: e.g., *in the room*; *in France*. This predicate simply indicates where something or somebody is. The following statements illustrate this predicate:

> The buses are *in the garage.*
>
> The cat is *on the window-sill.*
>
> Senator Kennedy was killed *in Los Angeles.*

(h) The accident of *posture* is a predicate that can be said of a subject as a result of that subject having a variety of *orderings of its parts in place*: e.g., leaning, stooping, crouching, reclining. This predicate expresses a notion quite different from that of place. Examples of this difference are numerous: such as the contents of a bottle of milk as it is transported from the creamery to the front-door steps of your home; a corpse that is transferred from Saigon to Seattle. The following statements illustrate this predicate:

> She was *reclining* on the sofa.
>
> As the monk burned, he was *kneeling.*
>
> He was *rather round-shouldered.*

(i) The accident of *dress* is a predicate that can be said of a subject that is clothed, armed, or in some way ornamented: e.g., *in his baseball uniform*; *in a bathing suit*. The following statements illustrate this predicate:

> Maureen looked exquisite *in her mantilla*.
>
> She appeared cool *in her evening gown*.
>
> The Marines were decked out *in their combat gear*.

IV

Throughout this analysis of predication we have tried to avoid falling into the trap of *psychologism*, a charge not infrequently made against logicians of the traditional school. Often such a charge is unfair because every theory of predication presupposes some theory of knowledge. No school of logic is neutral in its theory of predication. Logical positivism and the British analytical school tend to be Humean; traditional logicians tend to espouse the moderate realism of Aristotle.[9]

Aristotle's theory of predication presupposes two things: (1) that *words* are not the very things which they conventionally signify, i.e., the word dog does not bark or salivate; (2) that *concepts* are suprasensate images which can be both *universal* and *singular*, i.e., one can have an idea of human nature and also an idea of a human being, even one's self.

In this theory of knowledge, nothing is naturally germinated in the human intellect which is not in some way first in the senses. Conceptual thought is rooted in perceptual thought. Personal experience witnesses constantly that every normal human being is aware of his or her ability to understand that *relationship of oneness* which is so often found to be in and amongst individual entities. This *relationship of oneness* is traditionally referred to as a *universal*; hence we speak of a *dog* show or a *horse* show. Since words can be employed easily to signify such concepts of a universal nature in a meaningful way, none of us hesitate to make such statements as *some horses are brown* or *all dogs are animals*. A multidimensioned knowledge of this kind is an adequate and necessary source of normal meaningful predication, for infrahuman animals are by nature impotent to predicate, and singular predicates would be purposeless and needlessly repetitious: e.g., John Doe is John Doe.

Pertinent Quotations about the sources of predication:

(a)

Substance, in the truest and primary and most definite sense of the word, is that which is neither predicable of a subject nor present in a subject; for instance, the individual man or horse. But in a secondary sense those things are called substances within which, as *species*, the primary substances are included; also those which, as *genera*, include the species. For instance, the individual man is included in the species *man*, and the genus to which the species belongs is *animal*; these, therefore—that is to say, the species *man* and the genus *animal* —are termed secondary substances. . . .

Everything except primary substances is either predicable of a primary substance or present in a primary substance. This becomes evident by reference to particular instances which occur. *Animal* is predicated of the species *man,* therefore of the individual man, for if there were no individual man of whom it could be predicated, it could not be predicated of the species *man* at all. Again, colour is present in body, therefore in individual bodies, for if there were no individual body in which it was present, it could not be present in body at all. . . .

Further, primary substances are most properly so-called because they underlie and are the subjects of everything else. Now the same relation that subsists between primary substance and everything else subsists also between the *species* and the *genus* to which the primary substance belongs on the one hand, and every attribute which is not included within these on the other. For these are the subjects of all such attributes. If we call an individual man *skilled in grammar*, the predicate is applicable also to the species and to the genus to which he belongs. This law holds good in all cases . . . for a secondary substance is not an individual, but a *class* with a certain qualification;

for it is not one and single as a primary substance is; the words *man*, *animal*, are predicable of more than one subject.

Yet species and genus do not merely indicate quality, like the term *white*; *white* indicates quality and nothing further, but *species* and *genus* determine the quality with reference to a substance: they signify substance qualitatively differentiated. The determinate qualification covers a larger field in the case of the *genus* than in that of the *species*: he who uses the word *animal* is herein using a word of wider extension than he who uses the word *man*.

> —*The Basic Works of Aristotle*, tr. R. McKeon (New York: Random House, 1941), "Categories," ch. 5; by permission of the Clarendon Press, Oxford.

(b)

Moreover, that is said to be predicated essentially (*in quid*) which is a suitable response to the question, *what*?; as when it is said, *what is man*?, a suitable reply is *animal*. Thus *animal* is predicated of man essentially (*in quid*). Yet, in another way, genus itself is defined as *that under which species* is placed. Property, however, differs from accident because property is predicated about one species alone. Besides, accident is found prior in individuals and later in genera and species. After all, an animal or a man does not run, unless Socrates or Plato runs. Moreover, *property* is first in the species, and then through the species in singulars. Likewise, *genus, species, difference*, and *property* are equally shared by all about whom they are predicated; whereas, not so with *accident* but according to a more or less.

> —Peter of Spain, *Summulae Logicales*, tract II (author's translation).

(c)

God said, "Let the waters teem with living creatures, and let birds fly above the earth within the vault of heaven." And so it was. God created great sea serpents and every *kind* of living creature with which the waters teem, and every *kind* of winged creature. God saw that it was good.

> —Genesis I: 20–21 (*Jerusalem Bible*).

(d)

Thus the sentence is the order of words which become these words only by means of their very order. This is indeed what linguists and psychologists have perceived, and their embarrassment can be of use to us here as a counterproof; they believed that they discovered a circle in the formulation of speaking, for in order to speak it is necessary to know one's thought. But how can we know this thought as a reality made explicit and fixed in concepts except precisely by speaking it? Thus speech refers to thought and thought to speech. But we understand now that there is no circle or rather that this circle—from which linguists and psychologists believed they could escape by the invention of pure psychological idols such as the verbal image or an imageless, wordless thought—is not unique with speech; it is characteristic of the situation in general.

> —Jean Paul Sartre, *Being and Nothing-ness*, tr. H. E. Barnes (New York: Philosophical Library, 1956), p. 518.

(e)

The logical principle of genera, which postulates identity, is balanced by another principle, namely, that of *species*, which calls for mani-foldness and diversity in things, notwithstanding their agreement as coming under the same genus, and which prescribes to the under-standing that it attend to the diversity no less than to the identity. This principle (of discriminative observation, that is, of the faculty of distinction) sets a limit to possible indiscretion in the former principle, (of the faculty of wit); and reason thus exhibits a two-fold, self-conflicting interest, on the one hand interest in *extent* (universality) in respect of genera, and on the other hand in *content* (determinate-ness) in respect of the multiplicity of the species. In the one case the understanding thinks more *under* its concepts, in the other more *in* them. This two-fold interest manifests itself also among students of nature in the diversity of their ways of thinking. Those who are more especially speculative are, we may almost say, hostile to hetero-geneity, and are always on the watch for the unity of the genus; those, on the other hand, who are more especially empirical, are constantly endeavouring to differentiate nature in such manifold fashion as almost to extinguish the hope of ever being able to determine its appearances in accordance with universal principles.

> —Immanuel Kant, *Critique of Pure Reason*, tr. N. K. Smith (New York: St. Martin's Press, 1965), p. 540.

Exercise:

In the spaces provided, indicate the type of predication illustrated in each statement by using *S* for *essential* predication and *A* for *accidental,* then specify the category of the logical predicate employed.

(1) . . . . In the British Commonwealth the shilling is *legal tender.*

(2) . . . . Some animals are *bovine.*

(3) . . . . Not all lions are *brown.*

(4) . . . . Stephen is my *brother-in-law.*

(5) . . . . All men have the *ability to be grammatical.*

(6) . . . . Some dogs are *tripeds.*

(7) . . . . President Kennedy was killed *in Dallas.*

(8) . . . . All snowflakes are *white.*

(9) . . . . All oaks are *trees.*

(10) . . . . Some women are *superior to* others in cooking.

(11) . . . . Not all birds are *cardinals.*

(12) . . . . Some habits are *morally good.*

(13) . . . . She looked stunning *in her new evening gown.*

(14) . . . . The white hunter *shot* the elephant.

(15) . . . . The nuns spend hours *meditating.*

(16) . . . . Some basketball players are *seven feet tall.*

(17) . . . . He found her *drooped* over the couch.

(18) . . . . Not all airplanes are *elegantly shaped*.

(19) . . . . No cheetah is *slow*.

(20) . . . . Not all women are *lady-like*.

(21) . . . . Some virtues are *theological*.

(22) . . . . All men are *mammals*.

(23) . . . . Some geniuses are not *bearded*.

(24) . . . . Some cooks use *too much salt*.

(25) . . . . To err is *human*.

3

Definition and Predication

History is a witness to the phenomenon that men are ever concerned about bettering their modes of discourse. From the time of Plato and Aristotle up to the present, men have striven to make discourse more *meaningful*. Nevertheless, despite the advances in logic and semantics, ambiguity and vagueness in statements are still prevalent. Whenever statements lack clarity of meaning communication gaps result. We have recognized as members of society and as individuals that *meaningful* statements play a very important part in the universe of rational dialogue. Meaningful statements are those formed from *well-defined* terms.

Most logicians agree with Aristotle that many men are capable of formulating genuine definitions and that with their formulation precise predication becomes a real possibility. Scientists are quite aware that without well-defined terms sciences would be impossible, for genuine proofs would have no valid starting point. Satisfactory definitions, then, guarantee *meaning* in statements. In this chapter we shall consider the proper aims of valid or good definitions, their pattern of development, and some norms which they should satisfy.[1]

I

Perhaps, at first, it will be helpful to point out *what not to expect*
from a definition. No definition intends to establish the existence
of the set or group of things it is about to define (*definiendum*).
In the search for a thing's necessary elements, a thing's nature, it
is ordinarily assumed that these things *do exist* or *can exist* (i.e.,
that there is no inherent contradiction involved). Otherwise, it
is to search for nothing.

No definition is intended to be a proof, yet it is a necessary
beginning of the scientific process of proving. Very few definitions will signify the WHY of a thing; nor will they all take the
same shape of expression. Not every thing or every notion is
definable, either: e.g., the individual of a class (*this cow*); or the
concepts of unity and being. Though it must give some essential
information about the basic features of a thing, no definition
usurps the part of either an affirmative proposition or a negative
proposition; for, as Aristotle insists, in a definition one thing is
not predicated yet of another.[2]

What then should we expect from a definition? Every definition is meant to be an instrument for revealing something and in-
forming someone about a class or group or type of existential
(actual or possible) objects previously either unknown or un-
knowable. But it is a fact that definitions never come from
Nature already packaged, for Nature is most jealous about her
secrets. Yet definitions of real things are useless unless they are
rooted in empirical experience and based on inductive findings.
Ideally, *to define* is really nothing but an honest attempt to stake
out the proper claims of one class of entities from others similar
to it in some way: e.g., *justice*, among the moral virtues; *isosceles*,
among triangles; *silver*, among elemental metals; *man*, among
animals. To be able to discover the balance of *sameness* and
difference, objectively existing in classes of real or possible entities, is one of the more important requirements to be adept in
the art of constructing good definitions. To assist specialists in

all the fields of learning to form such definitions is properly the duty of the logician.

However, as we shall find, not all definitions are equally perfect formulas. Actually, the perfect definition is a formula signifying clearly and exactly the attributes necessarily present in a thing's essence or nature; for example, in *human nature*, which each man shares with his fellowman, animality and rationality are absolutely necessary elements, and no human nature could exist and be otherwise. The gradations of excellence among real definitions are determined simply by how adequately each reveals to us *what a thing is*.

Sometimes essences (that which makes a thing to be WHAT it is) are discovered through an analysis of their peculiar characteristics or properties. Perhaps more frequently, essences are made known to us by the experimental study of their accidents: e.g., color, valences, boiling or freezing points, molecular structure. The *approaches* devised by human ingenuity to uncover some of the secrets about the WHAT of natural things have been many and valuable: e.g., genetic, structural or morphological, taxonomic, and stipulative. The definitions offered in the sciences employing these approaches are helpful signs or instruments in manifesting the factors essential to many kinds of reality in the material world.[3] Each group of sciences (e.g., physics, psychology, mathematics, ethics) has its own indigenous *mode* of defining.

Aristotle is critical of those who think that substances alone can be defined. Accidents too are definable, "for even of a quality we might ask what it is, so that quality also is a *what a thing is*—not in the simple sense, however."[4] However, he does yield the priority of excellence to substantive definitions.

In the hierarchy of definitions, *nominal* ones hold the lowest place because they tend to manifest very little, if anything, of the noumenal elements of any class of entities: e.g., "biology" is derived from two Greek words, βιος meaning *life,* and λογος meaning *study of.* Naturally, this method of defining is quite unsatisfactory, especially so when one considers that definitions are only signs of things at best, not the things themselves.

II

Yet, despite all the ingenious approaches devised by man, satisfactory definitions are seldom easily come by. It is obviously unscientific to make defining a matter of guesswork. It is not a good pedagogical practice either to resort to procedures that are predominantly *a prioristic* (i.e., tailoring the objective reality to fit the definition). After all, oxygen is still oxygen regardless of our definitions of it. Offering or accepting mere *descriptions* of classes of entities as if they were genuine definitions, a not uncommon practice in many classrooms these days, is also open to serious challenge. The hard truth is that if a class of things is definable at all, then it is worth defining satisfactorily, even though that be—as it usually is—an arduous and complex task. The difficulty in forming definitions has been evident in decisions of the Courts about the notion of *decency* and its contrary, and in disputes about the scope of the terms *Jew* in Semitic circles and *the Church* among Christian groups. Even the definition of a phenomenon so common as *death* is an unsettled issue, yet a very important one ethically. In short, things of either a thoroughly material or immaterial nature have their own built-in handicaps for human investigation (e.g., arthropods and angels).

Searching for a valid definition is, then, usually a painstaking process. It is fundamentally a logical attempt to investigate into the core of being in which any entity or class of entities is grounded. Beginning with the study of individuals, an inductive investigation soon discloses their similarities and dissimilarities; then the investigation takes on many logical dimensions as species and genera are noticed.[5] Thus, it is clear that discovering and distinguishing are the tedious but indispensable steps in the formation of good definitions.

Perhaps because of the features of adventure and challenge so frequently associated with this phase of learning, Aquinas imaginatively compared the act of defining to hunting: an intellectual safari into the mysteries of being.[6] Successful defining is achieved only by a mind that can observe keenly the operational patterns of things, analyze and interpret consistently well the data observed, and recognize the various senses in which words or verbal signifiers can be employed. Only so equipped will one be proficient in the art of dissecting a notion, an object, or a problem with confidence and accuracy.

This was Plato's forte, as is evident in the *Dialogues*. It is a fact that Aristotle reverenced his teacher's uncanny ability to dissect or divide a subject. But he likewise criticized him for giving this process of learning too much emphasis.[7] Division certainly is an important phase in moving toward the formation of a definition. It surely is a necessary step in this scientific process that can terminate in demonstrative proof. But it is not an end in itself. This is said not in order to denigrate the process of division, but only to keep it in proper focus in the task of learning. In a word, logically correct divisions help immeasurably in the formulation of both satisfactory definitions and convincing arguments. To guarantee the successful making of valid definitions, Aristotle proposed *four* norms that all valid divisions should satisfy. Each of these norms will be separately analyzed:

Rule 1—Each part of any logical division must be less universal in its extension than the dividendum (that being divided). Translated into the physical order, this rule merely says that the tusks and legs of an elephant are not the whole elephant. *Logically*, it means that the notion of species is an attribute that is far more limited in the number of individuals to which it can be said to belong than the notion of genus: e.g., All tulips are plants; but, Not all plants are tulips. In other words, the number of individuals who belong to different kinds (species) within one and the same family (genus) varies inversely: there are many more things generically similar than there are in any species within that genus. Therefore, to include in a division a broader or a more extensive term than the *dividendum* would serve no useful purpose. For example, it is logically illicit to bring in the term "living" in dissecting the plant or animal kingdoms, or the term "element" in attempting to classify metals. This norm is a safe guide in the denotative approach to a definition.[8]

Rule 2—All the parts in the logical division must add up to and adequately exhaust the dividendum. This norm simply guarantees analytical completeness. To omit any part that is necessary to the integrity of a logical division is to court disaster in the treatment of any subject. How the demands of this canon are satisfied is illustrated in the classical division of "cardinal virtue" into prudence, justice, temperance, and fortitude. In the previous chapter the predicable "accident" also was divided in accordance with this logical rule. That every valid division or subdivision must have at least two parts seems to follow naturally, too, as a corollary from this logical norm, even though infractions of it are not uncommon. The following schema for an *outline* exemplifies faulty division:

A.

B.

    1.

        (a) . . . . either a (b) is added or this is absorbed in 1.

    2.

        (a)

        (b)

            (1) . . . . either a (2) is added or this is absorbed in (b).

Rule 3—The unicity of basis must be maintained throughout each division and/or subdivision. This rule demands that in each part of a logical division there be a sole frame of reference or point of view. Without fidelity to this norm, a division would be confusing and aimless for it would lack a unifying or cohesive factor. To shift arbitrarily the special basis of a division is to destroy its principle of order and comparison. In the concrete, the rule simply indicates that if one is to divide the notion "nationality," then its parts would properly be Indian, Canadian, Mexican, Kenyan, German, etc., while terms like rich, obese, learned, Protestant would be evidently irrelevant and would render the division logically unsound and literally incoherent.

Rule 4—Some basic opposition must exist between the parts of the division. This rule is of supreme importance insofar as it guarantees against all forms of overlapping or coalescence in a division. The parts of a logically correct division should be different, i.e., they should *clash* in some way. Since opposition means *the lack of identity between notions or things*, it is an efficient instrument for discriminating both real and ideal entities. In his *Metaphysics X*, Aristotle analyzes the four ways in which things can be said to be opposed:

(a) *Contradictory* opposition is the most fundamental type because it sets up a radical clash between any *positive* term or notion and its corresponding negation or total denial: e.g., European, non-European; veteran, nonveteran; metal, nonmetal; Semitic, non-Semitic; Bantu, non-Bantu; voter, nonvoter. This form of opposition is seldom the most informative, but it is always a safe way to begin the dissecting of a subject.

(b) *Contrary* opposition involves the greatest difference in the genus of opposition. It is that type of opposition which exists, usually, between two or more positive entities that are more or less the extremes of difference within one and the same genus. Unless all these conditions are verifiable, contraries will not result: e.g., *sourness*, in the order of taste, is not a genuine contrary of *at Athens*, in the order of place. This is an example of illicit leaping, as it were, from one category of being to another. The following contraries are valid: in motion, upward—downward; in number, odd—even; in color, red—green; in sound, loud—soft.

(c) *Privative* opposition is that type which can exist between the presence of a form and its lack in a subject that is naturally

capable of possessing that form. There are many examples of
privation: e.g., blindness in dogs; virtues in collegians; poverty
among people; lameness in horses. Sometimes privation is confused with what is really *negation*, and this identification could
occasion inexact statements. Negation is simply the lack of a
form or quality in an entity which is *naturally incapable of possessing it*: e.g., sight in a rock; the power to know in a plant; vice
in a cat.

(d) *Relative* opposition is that kind which can exist between
things, persons, and notions which are in some way associated
with one another or directed toward one another: e.g., students–
teacher; employees–employer; brothers–sisters; husband–wife;
children–parents.

III

From the analysis of division as a methodology in the genesis
and development of valid definitions, it should be clear that satisfactory definitions in every sphere of learning are not haphazardly
discovered. Neither are they arbitrarily formulated, once all the
data have been collated. Throughout the major works of Aristotle
four norms for producing good definitions constantly reappear.[9]
Over the centuries since his era, these canons or rules have
proved to be invaluable aids in the constructing of worthwhile
definitions. These are the *four* rules which no valid definition can
violate:

Rule 1—The definiendum (*the thing or notion to be defined*)
must be universal in character. Since the perfection of a definition
consists in being a formula in which the *essential ingredients*
of a notion or thing are signified, i.e., those elements without
which it is impossible for an entity to be of a special nature, this
logical rule excludes *singulars* from being able to be defined: it
excludes you, your father, your girl-friend's mother, your pet
dog, etc. Only something with a unicity of nature, i.e., some
entity that has a real substantial unity, lends itself to the perfec-

tion looked for in a definition, for definition is primarily of a thing's substantive form (that which makes it to be what it is). In short, definitions are chiefly concerned with the *whatness* of a class of entities, not their *thisness*.

Negatively, too, this rule implies that definitions of complex entities (e.g., brown bear, white motel, academic freedom, round bronze) always tend to be confused and ambiguous. Regardless of whether a circle is small or large, cast in wood or glass or iron, its genuine definition will express only the essence of circularity, and essences are characteristically *universal*; examples of essences are man, justice, crustacea, oxygen, dentistry.

Rule 2—Every definition should strive to contain an entity's generic likeness and its specific differential. This rule spells out the necessary features or contents of the universal notion that is about to be defined, i.e., its quiddity or essence. In the previous chapter we said that *genus* is the category that enables us to predicate the same thing of a number of things that have much in common but at the same time exhibit profound *differences in kind*, i.e., essential or radical factors that make them more than accidentally distinctive. Generic likenesses in things are usually more apparent to us than their differences because of their complete corporeal makeup, as is evident among classes of birds, of fishes, and of metals. Nevertheless both these factors of the definiendum (genus and specific difference) in each instance must be contained in the definition.

One sure way to fulfill this rule is by zeroing in on the *proximate genus* of a class of things (e.g., horse in relation to animal, or habit in relation to quality). By such a move the definition that results will naturally be more exact and more manifestive. Insofar as a thing's intrinsic principle of *otherness* among entities with which it shares a common likeness can be discovered, the necessary reason for its distinctiveness in the class can be made clear in the definition. Aristotle put it more simply: "there is nothing in the definition except the first-named genus and the differentiae."[10]

Rule 3—The definition and the definiendum ought to be convertible. This rule is really more of a method of checking the perfection of a definition already formulated; in fact, it is the easiest and most effective way to test the validity of a definition. As a rule-of-thumb, it means simply that the definiendum and its proper definition should be *interchangeable* in all instances of predication.

In the concrete, the rule means that wherever the term *sin* is employed in statements, the term *a morally bad action* can be equally substituted. Other illustrations are: *virtue*, good habit; *man*, rational animal; *vice*, a morally bad habit. Sometimes even the truly peculiar property of a class of entities will satisfy this condition in predication: e.g., *man*, a risible being or tool-making animal. As we shall see in a later chapter, modern logicians also use a procedure something like this and call it *interdefinability*.[11]

Rule 4—The definition ought to signify more clearly than the definiendum. This logical rule preserves the very purpose of a definition: to dissipate the vagueness surrounding a term. Clarity of meaning is ordinarily guaranteed in definitions if *univocal* terms are employed. A *univocal* term is one which is imposed on many different things, but signifying the very same nature (generic or specific) in each: e.g., as *animal* can be similarly said of men and oxen; as *student* in relation to freshmen and seniors; as *science*, of chemistry and sociology and mathematics.[12]

Any definition will be lacking in clarity if it tends to be circular, equivocal, or metaphorical. As is evident in dictionaries, lexicographers are prone to give *circular* definitions, for they often include words in a definition which are in the definiendum itself: e.g., dentist, one who practices dentistry; traveler, one who travels. Whether they are meant to be or not, such definitions are not very informative about the essential notes of substances or accidents.

An *equivocal* term is one that happens to be imposed on many things which have completely different natures that are not really related. They are related *nominally* insofar as the same term is applied to different things. But their meanings are poles apart: e.g., *coaches*, applied to athletic personnel and railroad cars; *pen*, applied to a writing instrument and a fenced-in area for pigs. *Equivocation* is found in most languages and makes puns and jokes possible. However, double-talk is never tolerated in definitions. *Metaphors* are also dangerous in definitions. Regardless of how skillfully metaphors or other figures of speech can be used, they generally tend to interfere with the clarity of definitions insofar as they call attention to themselves and use verbal signifiers in transferred senses. At best, they should be employed only to exemplify or to illustrate the meaning of terms used in a definition.

Circumstances may warrant, however, the use of *analogous* terms in a logically correct definition. This situation occurs not infrequently in most sciences. An *analogous* term is one that by design is imposed upon many objects signifying quite distinct formalities or natures in each, yet in some way similarly related: as when the term *healthy* is attributed to animals, food, and complexion; or the term *being* is predicated of both creatures and the Creator. Whenever the entities to be defined are either infrahuman or suprahuman, analogous terms are to be expected in genuine definitions.

Finally, we should note that this fourth rule does permit a great amount of *relativity* in the formulation of a definition. This is so because of the variety of possible reasons for constructing it in the first place. Technical terms are appropriate in a definition intended for scholars and specialists; but they should be avoided if the definition is framed for a less demanding purpose. Since meaningfulness is always so subjectively conditioned, definitions should be couched in language with which the intended audience is more or less familiar, for whatever is received is always received according to the mode and capacity of the receiver.

Having completed our examination of the ingredients necessary for predication, we can move on to the study of predication itself, which will take up the remaining chapters of this book.

Pertinent Quotations about both division and definition:

(a)

The *champion of division* (i.e., Plato) might here urge that though these lapses do occur, yet we can solve that difficulty if all the attributes we assume are constituents of the definable form, and if, postulating the genus, we produce by division the requisite uninterrupted sequence of terms, and omit nothing; and that indeed we cannot fail to fulfill these conditions if what is to be divided falls whole into the division at each stage, and none of it is omitted; and that this—the dividendum—must without further question be (ultimately) incapable of fresh specific division. Nevertheless, we reply, division does not involve inference; if it gives knowledge, it gives it another way.

> —*The Basic Works of Aristotle*, tr. R. McKeon (New York: Random House, 1941), "Posterior Analytics II," ch. 5; by permission of the Clarendon Press, Oxford.

(b)

Theatetus: I suspect that we have now discovered the object of our search.

Stranger: Then now you and I have come to an understanding not only about the name of the angler's art, but about the definition of the thing itself. One half of all art was acquisitive—half of the acquisitive art was conquest or taking by force; half of this was hunting, and half of hunting was hunting animals, half of this was hunting water animals; of this again, the under half was fishing, half of fishing was striking; a part of striking was fishing with a barb, and one half of this again, being the kind which strikes with a hook and draws the fish from below upwards, is the *art* which we have been seeking, and which from the nature of the operation is denoted *angling* or drawing up.

Theatetus: The result has been quite satisfactorily brought out.

> —Plato, *Dialogues*, "The Sophist," tr.
> B. Jowett (New York: Random House,
> 1937).

(c)

It is useful to have examined the *number of meanings* of a term both for clearness' sake (for a man is more likely to know what it is he asserts, if it has been made clear to him how many meanings it may have), and also with a view to ensuring that our reasonings shall be in accordance with the actual facts and not addressed merely to the term used. For as long as it is not clear in how many senses a term is used, it is possible that the answerer and the questioner are not directing their minds upon the same thing: whereas when once it has been made clear how many meanings there are, and also upon which of them the former directs his mind when he makes his assertion, the questioner would then look ridiculous if he failed to address his argument to this. It helps us also both to avoid being misled and to mislead by false reasoning.

> —*The Basic Works of Aristotle*, tr. R.
> McKeon (New York: Random House,
> 1941), "Topics I," ch. 18; by permission
> of the Clarendon Press, Oxford.

(d)

When you *define* the beautiful as that which has its teleology in itself and adduce by way of illustration a young girl or nature or a work of art, I can make nothing out of it but that the whole rant about all these things having their teleology in themselves is an illusion. If there is to be any question of teleology there must be a movement, for as soon as I think of a goal I think of a movement; even when I think of one who is at the goal I think of a movement, for I reflect that he has reached it by a movement. What you call *beautiful* manifestly lacks movement; for the beautiful in nature simply *is*; and when I view a work of art and penetrate its thought with my thought, it is really in me the movement occurs, not in the work of art. It may be you are right in saying that the beautiful has its teleology in itself, but as you construe this definition and employ it, it is no more than a negative expression which signifies that the beautiful has not its teleology in anything else.

—Søren Kierkegaard, *Either/Or*, trans. by D. F. and L. M. Swenson (Princeton, N.J.: Princeton University Press, 1944), p. 278.

(e)

Some writers propose to reach the definitions of the ultimate forms of animal life by bipartite division. But this method is often difficult, and often impracticable.

Sometimes the final differentia of the subdivision is sufficient by itself, and the antecedent differentiae are mere surplusage. Thus in the series Footed, Two-footed, Cleft-footed, the last term is all-expressive by itself, and to append the higher terms is only an idle iteration.

Again it is not permissible to break up a natural group, Birds for instance, by putting its members under different bifurcations, as is done in the published dichotomies, where some birds are ranked with animals of the water, and others placed in a different class. The group Birds and the group Fishes happen to be named, while other natural groups have no popular names; for instance, the groups that we may call Sanguineous and Bloodless are not known popularly by any designations. If such natural groups are not to be broken up, the method of Dichotomy cannot be employed, for it necessarily involves such breaking up and dislocation. The group of the Many-footed, for instance, would, under this method, have to be dismembered, and some of its kinds distributed among land animals, others among water animals.

—*The Basic Works of Aristotle*, tr. R. McKeon (New York: Random House, 1941), "On the Parts of Animals," ch. 2; by permission of the Clarendon Press, Oxford.

(f)

In order to *formulate* the connexions we wish to prove we have to select our analyses and divisions. The method of selection consists in

laying down the common genus of all our subjects of investigation
—if e.g., they are animals, we lay down what the properties are
which inhere in every animal. These established, we next lay down
the properties essentially connected with the first of the remaining
classes—e.g., if this first sub-genus is bird, the essential properties of
every bird—and so on, always characterizing the proximate sub-
genus. This will clearly at once enable us to say in virtue of what
character the sub-genera—man, e.g., or horse—possess their properties. Let A be animal, B the properties of every animal, C. D, E,
various species of animal. Then it is clear in virtue of what character
B inheres in D—namely, A—and that it inheres in C and E for the
same reason: and throughout the remaining sub-genera always the
same rule applies.

—*The Basic Works of Aristotle*, tr. R.
McKeon (New York: Random House,
1941), "Posterior Analytics II," ch. 14;
by permission of the Clarendon Press,
Oxford.

Exercises:

On Division:

(1) Taking the the terms *government, art, education, law, mammal,* attempt to construct a valid division of each, extending each division to at least four subdivisions.

(2) *Evaluate* these divisions as *valid* or *invalid* in the light of the four basic rules for validity; if *invalid*, state the rule most directly violated:

(a) .... *Lecture*: technical, interesting, expensive, nontechnical

(b) .... *Language*: Romance, Greek, Aramaic, dead, Swahili, French

(c) .... *Hospital personnel*: workers, patients on the danger list, unskilled, doctors, patients not on the danger list, nurses, skilled

(d) .... *People*: poor, rich, good, animal, bad, middle-class

(e) .... *Music*: operatic, nonoperatic

(f) .... *Family*: parents, in-laws, children, grandparents, those who have reached puberty, those who have not reached puberty

(g) .... *American military forces*: Navy, Air Force, Coast Guard, Army, Marines

(h) .... *Arthropoda*: crustacea, insecta, arachnids, centipedes, and millipedes

(i) . . . . *Sound*: loud, soft

(j) . . . . *Theological virtue*: faith, hope, habit, charity.

On Definition:

Evaluate these alleged definitions as *valid* or *invalid*; if *invalid*, state the rule most directly violated:

(a) . . . . *Jomo Kenyatta*, first Prime Minister of Kenya

(b) . . . . *Man*, an animal capable of being a musician

(c) . . . . *Wedding-ring*, a nuptial tourniquet cutting off circulation

(d) . . . . *Sociology*, a generalizing science of sociocultural phenomena viewed in their generic forms, types and manifold connections (P. Sorokin)

(e) . . . . *Grammarian*, one who is expert in grammar

(f) . . . . *Triangle*, a plane figure bounded by three straight lines

(g) . . . . *Sacrament*, an external symbol instituted by Christ for salvation

(h) . . . . *Knife*, an instrument used for cutting

(i) . . . . *Vanity*, an exaggerated good opinion of oneself grounded in self-love

(j) . . . . *Motion*, an act of being in potency qua potency.

4

Propositions and Predication

Semanticists and logicians are in general agreement that language can have many purposes. One of them is to make *informative* statements: e.g., It is raining; Some pickles are sweet. They also agree that, regardless of its purpose, a statement with well-defined terms ought to be clear and meaningful.

But, as we have seen, terms or words are *not* statements in themselves. They are simply symbols signifying a concept or a special kind of entity, with no explicit relationship to another concept or other kind of thing. Then, too, definitions are not statements either, no matter how exact they may be. In short, individual words or even series of words, whether arranged in order alphabetically (e.g., ants, artichokes, attack) or haphazardly juxtaposed (e.g., big, Indians, cows, shoot), can lack the necessary ingredients of a genuinely meaningful statement.

I

To be *meaningful*, a statement should be a unity of symbols that expresses something *about* something or somebody, or *to* something or somebody, or *for* something or somebody: e.g., Are all cooks fat?; Some animals are not carnivorous; Let us pray to the

Lord; Quick, Chauncey, the vermouth! Yet, without such verbal signifiers (and non-verbal ones in some sciences) meaningful statements would be impossible to construct.

Though words and terms can, by themselves, signify ideas and objects, it must be remembered that they ordinarily do not signify whether or not these ideas or objects actually exist, or whether they are related to or connected with each other, i.e., whether attribute A belongs or does not belong, accidentally or nonaccidentally, to idea or object B. In brief, words especially are highly limited in their signification and meaningfulness because by themselves they are *neither affirmations nor negations*. Affirmations and negations are the most basic forms of predication: e.g., Some girls *are* pretty; Some girls *are not* pretty. No verbal or non-verbal signifiers, purely by themselves, are formal or full-fledged statements. Nevertheless, words and terms are the essential elements of all predications, i.e., they make predication possible.

However, unlike grammarians, logicians are really interested in only one kind of predication, one type of meaningful statement. It is traditionally known as the *proposition*. In this chapter we shall make a logical analysis (1) of the notion of *supposition*, which is basic to all types of predication, and (2) of the nature of the *proposition* insofar as it is a special kind of informative predication. In the next chapter we shall turn our attention to the various types of propositions from which all arguments employing verbal signifiers are constructed.

II

What, then, is *supposition*? It is most closely associated with the basic signification or meaning of each word used in a statement. Very simply, it can be said that *supposition* (sometimes called *designation*) is the proximate reason for words or terms serving the roles of *subject* and *predicate* in any meaningful statement. However, without the basic meaning of words being preserved, statements would be meaningless or even ridiculous. Then rational discourse would become an impossibility.

With many other savants Aristotle agrees that *subject* and *predicate* are the essential factors of any meaningful statement, especially a proposition. In other words, he looked upon the subject and predicate of any proposition as *slots* or *frames* into which verbal signifiers could indefinitely be placed to express a relationship of belonging or not belonging between entities and their attributes:

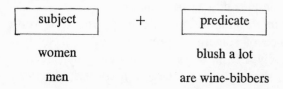

subject	+	predicate
women		blush a lot
men		are wine-bibbers

Meaningful statements are still formulated along these lines. Regardless of the intended or nonintended function of a statement—for sometimes the purely informative statement can become emotive or even directive—there is a subject-predicate relationship reflected in some way in every meaningful statement or sentence. Sometimes, as in commands and prayers, the subject may be anonymous or suppressed or even taken for granted: e.g., (you) Halt!; (Steve) Come here! (you) Shoot (him)!; (Lord) Forgive me. Sometimes the predicate is merely a simple form of the verb *is* or *is not*: e.g., John is; John is not. At other times, the predicate contains other parts of speech besides the verb: e.g., Not all ecumenists *are Christians*: Some people *speak quickly*. However, any further analysis along these lines serves no worthwhile purpose in logic, for all meaningful statements have a subject and a predicate; the proposition is no exception.

Supposition has been traditionally divided into two general types or classes, *improper* and *proper,* each with its own salient characteristics:

(a) *Improper supposition* consists in the use of a word in a statement in such a way that its metaphorical or nonliteral meaning is expressed: e.g., the reference to Christ as Lamb of God or Lion of Juda, as in the sentence "The Lamb of God is merciful"; or the reference to Joe DiMaggio as the Yankee Clipper in the sentence "The Yankee Clipper kills the Tigers."

(b) *Proper supposition* consists in the use of a word in a statement in such a way that its literal or real meaning is expressed; the word *mice* is so used in the following sentences: "Some mice are cheese-eaters"; "Some pets are mice." In these examples the word signifies a special type of animal nature in the proximate genus *rodent*. Proper supposition can be conveniently subdivided into (1) simple and (2) personal.

(1) *Simple* supposition is the employment of words to signify the essence of something precisely and exclusively as it exists conceptually, i.e., in one's mind without any reference to the individuals sharing it: e.g., *Dog* is a species; *Animal* is a genus; *Color* is an accident.

(2) *Personal* supposition is the use of words to signify both a nature and those entities that share it: e.g., in the statement "Man is an animal" the term *man* refers both to the human nature and to all individuals who share it.

In order to avoid confusion this division of *supposition* has been kept simple. In no way is it intended to appear as an exhaustive division. For the sake of completeness only, however, it might be feasible to mention here that, because the so-called *material* supposition does not refer in any way to the meaning of a verbal signifier, its logical value is minimal. In a nutshell, material supposition is the use of a word or term in a statement merely to represent itself: e.g., "Talking is a seven letter word": "Dog is a monosyllabic symbol."

This analysis of the logical property known as *supposition* provides us with the necessary orientation we will need when we turn to the study of the *proposition* itself. It was intended to be only a functional analysis. Before our formal study of the proposition itself, not a little credit should be given to some of the medieval thinkers for their insights about the scope of supposition. Reputable historians of logic have recognized the excellence of these insights as both unique and original contributions to logic.[1] Finally, as we shall see in later chapters, a shift in an argument from one kind or level of supposition to another, whether done knowingly or not, is a common mode of fallacious reasoning.

III

Aristotle's *ex professo* or *formal* treatment of PROPOSITION can be found in the work known as *On Interpretation*.[2] It is from the early chapters of this small book that the traditional definition of proposition has been formulated, viz: *a perfect composite expression that signifies a judgment and declares something to be true or false.* Each major part of this definition merits examination.

(a) Logicians are in agreement that every "composite expression" is an orderly grouping of words whose parts are capable of signifying something separately: e.g., to the opera house; Pope Paul VI is now reigning. Such utterances are evidently quite different from the simple word or term, such as *dog* or *hyena*. In the definition of proposition just stated, however, the term "composite expression" is not the proximate genus, because composite expressions can be either *perfect* or *imperfect*.

Unless a composite expression generates or translates a complete or total meaning, it is considered *imperfect*: e.g., "If Jack Kennedy had not been in Dallas that Friday"; "When the American generals were nearing Berlin." Such assertions are obviously incomplete in their meaning, simply because they keep one in suspense about what is omitted. On the other hand, the *perfect* composite expression conveys a complete meaning to the mind of the hearer or reader: e.g., "Where are you going?"; "Not all habits are virtues."; "Some houses are expensive." Grammarians call such statements *independent sentences*.

Handbooks of grammar commonly divide *independent sentences* (or *perfect composite expressions*) into four conventional types or classes: interrogative, exclamatory, imperative, and declarative. Grammarians remind us that, though the chief purpose of each of these general types or classes is set, they are flexible enough to serve other functions occasionally. However, each type or class naturally has a special or unique function to serve in ordinary discourse. The *interrogative* sentence performs the function of questioning or inquiring: "Where are you hiding the loot?", "Who is pitching today?", "When did George Boole live?". The *exclamatory* sentences generally take the form of prayers or emotional outbursts: "O King, lover of men!", "Lord, save us, we perish!", "Wow, what a shot that was!". The *imperative* sentence naturally tends to express requests or commands: "Shape up or ship out.", "Keep this door locked at all times.", "Don't shoot till you see the whites of their eyes." The *declarative* sentence is generally used to announce something or to express some information about something: "The Red Sox have won seven straight ball games.", "He likes your new hat.", "She had a very nice time at the junior prom." Of these four grammatical types or classes, it is with the *declarative* sentence that the *proposition* has the greatest affinity.

Yet not all declarative sentences are propositions or are intended to be propositions. Only those declarative sentences are propositions that (1) signify a judgment and (2) possess a *truth-value*, i.e., are either true or false. These two elements are indispensable parts of every genuine proposition and serve to distinguish the proposition within the class of declarative sentence, which is its *proximate* genus. In short, then, a proposition is a special kind or type of *perfect composite expression*.

(b) Unlike a word, which is limited and isolated in its role as a signifier, a proposition by nature signifies one or another form of *relationship* between concepts and/or objects. It represents a kind of comparative study between them, an attempt to discover whether or not they are in some ways *compatible*. Every genuine proposition is a sign that has some reference to a comparison. If a *compatibility* is perceived to exist, actually or possibly, between two or more entities, it is signified by an *affirmative* statement, i.e., a proposition that expresses some kind of composition: e.g., Some ducks are white; All men are mammals; Some x belong to y. If, on the other hand, an *incompatibility* is perceived to exist, actually or possibly, between two or more entities, it is signified by a *negative* statement, i.e., a proposition that expresses some kind of separation or division: e.g., Not all ducks are white; Some mammals are not men; All x do not belong to y. These *relationships* are cognitive phenomena frequently experienced by each of us and are grounded in transsubjective reality.

In a sense, each of us in such cognitive experiences acts like a *judge* in a courtroom, for we do make a decision about the factual datum presented to us. We do pass *judgment* on whether or not some attribute belongs to something. But, prior to our manifesting this judgment externally in the form of a propositional statement, an *internal decision* has already been made. Propositions, then, represent a judgment about the agreement or disagreement between two or more concepts and/or things. In short, a proposition is nothing else than an artificial or conventional sign of a mental judgment about the relationship between two or more entities.

A proposition, then, that is to be meaningful must be a sign that mirrors this internal judgment about the objective agreement or disagreement between two or more entities. As we saw earlier, the proposition, like all meaningful statements, is composed essentially of two parts, the *subject-term* and the *predicate-term*. Each part we described as a *slot* into which verbal signifiers are placed to express the relationship of agreement or disagreement between two or more entities.

Traditionally in logic, these two terms have been called the *extremes* of the proposition. The subject-term is usually *substantive* in character, for it is *that about which* something is to be predicated as belonging to it or not: Some dogs are smart; Not all cops are brutal; Some hippies are effeminate; All voters in Boston are not Democrats. On the other hand, the predicate-term has the job of describing the subject-term, by attributing some perfection or imperfection to it with the help of some form of the verb *to be* or one of its numerous syntactic equivalents: e.g., Some cooks *are good*; All cooks *are not garlic-users*; Some priests *watch for birds* (i.e., *are birdwatchers*). We will have occasion to use the word *extremes* frequently, in the special sense we have just given it, in referring to the subject-term and predi-cate-term of a proposition.

(c) As *signs of judgments* grounded in objective reality, propositions are tied closely with *truth-values*. A proposition has a *true* truth-value if and only if what it expresses is satisfied by all the entities to which it refers; otherwise, a proposition is said to have a *false* truth-value. For Aristotelians, objective evidence is the most neutral norm of satisfaction by which the truth-value of a proposition can be judged. Recognition of the relationship of objective compatibility or noncompatibility between two or more entities is required before we can make either a meaning-ful affirmative proposition or a meaningful negative proposition. If a propositional statement affirms an attribute of something that objectively does not possess it, the proposition simply has a *false* truth-value. So also, if a proposition denies an attribute of something that does objectively possess it, the proposition simply has a *false* truth-value. On the other hand, a propositional state-ment that affirms an attribute of something which objectively does possess it simply has a *true* truth-value. And a proposition that denies an attribute belongs to something which objectively does not possess it also has a *true* truth-value. Unless something to the contrary is said, it is generally accepted that an individual proposition is meant to be true, or to have a true truth-value. No genuine proposition, then, will be without either truth-value; neither will a genuine proposition have both truth-values simul-taneously.

Though logicians are not chiefly interested in the truth of things that fall outside the scope of logic, as was pointed out in the introduction, they are keenly interested in the truth of propo-sitions and the part truth plays in integral argumentation. In a later chapter we shall see that logicians today have not so much a disregard for logical truth as a greater interest in its functional uses (e.g., in testing the validity of inferences by truth-tables).

It should now be clear that a *proposition* is a special kind of declarative sentence; it is a significant statement asserting some-thing to be true or false. In the next chapter we shall examine the different *kinds* of propositions.

Pertinent Quotations about the nature of propositions:

(a)

As there are in the mind thoughts which do not involve truth or falsity, and also those which must be either true or false, so it is in speech. For truth and falsity imply combination and separation. Nouns and verbs, provided nothing is added, are like thoughts without combination or separation; *man* and *white*, as isolated terms, are not yet either true or false. In proof of this consider the word *goat-stag*. It has significance, but there is no truth or falsity about it, unless *is* or *is not* is added, either in the present or in some other tense.

By a *noun* we mean a sound significant by convention which has no reference to time, and of which no part is significant apart from the rest. In the noun, *fairsteed*, the part *steed* has no significance in and by itself, as in the phrase, *fairsteed*. Yet there is a difference between simple and composite nouns; for in the former the part is in no way significant; in the latter it contributes to the meaning of the whole, although it has not an independent meaning. Thus in the word, *pirate-boat*, the word *boat* has no meaning except as part of the whole word.

> —*The Basic Works of Aristotle*, tr. R. McKeon (New York: Random House, 1941), "On Interpretation," ch. 1 and 2; by permission of the Clarendon Press, Oxford.

(b)

The question, famed of old, by which logicians were supposed to be driven into a corner, obliged either to have recourse to a pitiful sophism, or to confess their ignorance and consequently the emptiness of their whole art, is the question: What is truth? The nominal definition of truth, that it is the agreement of knowledge with its object, is assumed as granted; the question asked is as to what is the general and sure criterion of the truth of any and every knowledge.

To know what questions may reasonably be asked is already a great and necessary proof of sagacity and insight. For if a question is absurd in itself and calls for an answer where none is required, it not only brings shame on the propounder of the question, but may betray an incautious listener into absurd answers, thus presenting, as the ancients said, the ludicrous spectacle of one man milking a he-goat and the other holding a sieve underneath.

If truth consists in the agreement of knowledge with its object, that object must thereby be distinguished from other objects; for knowledge is false, if it does not agree with the object to which it is related, even although it contains something which may be valid of other objects. Now a general criterion of truth must be such as would be valid in each and every instance of knowledge, however their objects may vary. It is obvious however that such a criterion (being general) cannot take account of the (varying) content of knowledge (relation to its specific object). But since truth concerns just this very content, it is quite impossible, and indeed absurd, to ask for a general test of the truth of such content. A sufficient and at the same time general criterion of truth cannot possibly be given. Since we have already entitled the content of knowledge its matter, we must be prepared to recognize that of the truth of knowledge, so far as its matter is concerned, no general criterion can be demanded. Such a criterion would by its very nature be self-contradictory.

—Immanuel Kant, *Critique of Pure Reason*, tr. N. K. Smith (2.3 "Transcendental Doctrine of Elements" (New York: St. Martin's Press, 1965), pp. 97–98.

(c)

Just as the true is found primarily in the intellect rather than in things, so also is it found primarily in an act of the intellect *joining and separating*, rather than in an act by which it forms the quiddities of things. For the nature of the true consists in a conformity of thing and intellect. Nothing becomes conformed with itself, but conformity requires distinct terms. Consequently, the nature of truth is first found in the intellect when the intellect begins to possess something proper to itself, not possessed by the thing outside the soul, yet corresponding to it, so that between the two—intellect and thing—a conformity may be found. In forming the quiddities of things, the intellect merely has a *likeness* of a thing existing outside the soul, as a sense has a likeness when it receives the species of a sensible thing.

But when the intellect begins *to judge* about the thing it has apprehended, then its *judgment* is something proper to itself—not something found outside in the thing. And the *judgment* is said to be *true* when it conforms to the external reality. Moreover, the intellect judges about the thing it has apprehended at the moment when it *says that something is or is not*. This is the role of *the intellect composing and dividing*.

> —St. Thomas Aquinas, *On Truth*, quest. I, art. 3, p. 13, tr. R. W. Mulligan (Chicago: H. Regnery Co., 1952).

(d)

Moreover supposition and signification differ, because signification is through the imposition of the word on the thing to be signified; *supposition*, in fact, is the acceptance of the term itself already signifying the thing for another, as when it is said, *man is running*. That term, *man*, is in place of Socrates or Plato or of any others. Wherefore, signification is prior to supposition, and they are not the same, because *to signify* is of a *sound*; whereas to *suppose* is truly of a *term* already composed of a sound and signification. Therefore, supposition is not signification . . . ; *personal* supposition is the acceptance of a common term for its own inferiors, as when it is said, *man runs*, where the term *man* is in place of individuals such as Socrates, Plato, and any others.

> —Peter of Spain, *Summulae Logicales*, Tract VI (*On Supposition*); Marietti edit., (author's translation).

(e)

Fourscore and seven years ago our fathers brought forth on this continent a new nation, conceived in Liberty, and dedicated to the proposition that all men are created equal.

> —*Documents of American History*, "The Gettysburg Address," edit. H. S. Commager (New York: Appleton-Century-Crofts, Inc., 1948), 4th edit., pp. 428–429.

(f)

The expression *This is the chalice of My blood* is a figure of speech, which can be understood in two ways. First, as a figure of metonymy; because the container is put for the contained, so that the meaning is: *This is My blood contained in the chalice*; of which mention is now made, because Christ's blood is consecrated in this sacrament, inasmuch as it is the drink of the faithful, which is not implied under the notion of blood; consequently this had to be denoted by the vessel adapted for such usage.

Secondly, it can be taken by way of metaphor, so that Christ's Passion is understood by the chalice by way of comparison, because, like a cup, it inebriates, according to Lam. iii. 15: *He hath filled me with bitterness, he hath inebriated me with wormwood*: hence our Lord Himself spoke of His Passion as a chalice, when He said (Matt. xxvi 39): *Let this chalice pass away from Me*:—so that the meaning is: *This is the chalice of My Passion*. This is denoted by the blood being consecrated apart from the body; because it was by the Passion that the blood was separated from the body.

> —St. Thomas Aquinas, *Summa Theo-
> logica*, part III, quest. 78, art. 3, ad 1,
> tr. Fathers of the English Dominican Prov-
> ince (New York: Benziger Bros., 1947),
> vol. II, p. 2475.

Exercise:

In the spaces provided before the following *composite expressions*, identify each as either *perfect* or *imperfect*; if *perfect*, further specify whether it is a genuine proposition.

(1) . . . . To the big and cloud-covered Ngong hills.

(2) . . . . While Rome was burning.

(3) . . . . All Africans are not black.

(4) . . . . Put up or shut up!

(5) . . . . Holy hat, someone shot grandmother!

(6) . . . . Black cat.

(7) . . . . Every cognitive action is pleasurable.

(8) . . . . If the Red Sox keep winning this season.

(9) . . . . Either you will drink your Scotch.

(10) . . . . Some agnostics are amoral.

(11) . . . . Not all ecdysiasts are pretty.

(12) . . . . Are you older than your brother?

(13) . . . . In a little Spanish town.

(14) . . . . No logicians are passionate.

(15) . . . . L. B. Johnson was president of the U.S.A.

(16) . . . . Quick, Henry, the Flit.

(17) . . . . All the U. S. astronauts are not sharp businessmen.

(18) . . . . How I would love to go on an African safari!

(19) .... All Canadians are not French.

(20) .... Some bus-drivers are polite.

(21) .... Would you like some more coffee?

(22) .... Nothing is absolute.

(23) .... If I had sunk that putt.

(24) .... Evolution is an ascent toward conscious-
ness.

(25) .... No nonveterans are nonvoters.

5

Kinds of Propositions

Our chief objective in this chapter will be to attempt a panoramic survey of the domain of propositions. This is expedient because not all propositional statements are of the same logical kind; as a matter of fact, there may be profound differences between one proposition and another. By becoming familiar with the general types or classes of propositions we will broaden our knowledge of this important logical entity and also make clear the dimensions of its inferential role in discourse.

Most people are unaware that they ordinarily speak and write with a form of statement that is reducible to the form of a proposition. If anyone attempts to assert something about something, and if this assertion is either true or false, one is communicating by means of a *proposition*.

Like styles of dress and coiffure, the logical shape of propositional statements can vary in many ways; diction may be technical or informal, syntax may be simple or complex, etc. Yet underneath the many possibilities of style in discourse, all propositional statements have certain common features, as we saw in the previous chapter.

In this chapter, then, we shall consider a functional theme that should make possible an accurate yet simple classification of all propositions. Doubtless we shall need to oversimplify the matter somewhat, but there is no point in carrying the classification of propositions further than will be useful to us at present. In this functional study of propositions, therefore, we shall consider only three general types or classes: the *categorical*, the *noncategorical*, and the *modal*.

I

The *categorical* proposition is a simple truth-value statement signifying a single intellectual judgment. Some logicians are inclined to call this type of proposition *atomic*.[1] Signifying either a composition or a division, the categorical proposition in its standardized form consists of two extremes: a subject-term, and a predicate term of which the verb-copula is an essential part (e.g., Some teachers of biology are nuns; All nurses are not overpaid). It is actually the *verb-copula* (i.e., some form of the verb *to be*) that indicates the way the rest of the predicate-term is related to the subject-term: e.g., Some apples *are* rotten; Some apples *are not* rotten. This factor is the basis for the profound *qualitative* difference between categorical propositions, i.e., whether they are affirmative or negative.[2]

(a)

All categorical propositions are either *affirmative* or *negative*, as we shall presently see, depending upon whether they reflect *composition* or *division*, respectively, between their own extremes.

An *affirmative* proposition is a positive statement, a proposition in which the attribute in the predicate-term is asserted to belong to and is joined with the subject-term. Some sort of combination of, or connection between the extremes of the proposition is always evident: e.g., Some animals are vertebrates; Man is fallible; All citizens are patriotic.

A *negative* proposition is one in which the attribute in the predicate-term is asserted to be cut off or separated in some way from its subject-term. In other words, connection between the extremes of the proposition is denied: e.g., Christ was not an imposter; Some sailors did not reenlist; No virtues are vices.

The problem of identifying the *quality* of categorical propositions can be, at first, a very difficult one for students of logic. It is understandably puzzling to learn that though some categorical propositions have an *apparently positive* verb-copula, they are properly regarded as *negative*: e.g., Not all taxpayers *are* whites; No arsonist *is* a law-abiding citizen. However, ordinarily, if a categorical proposition has an *apparently positive* verb-copula, and if there is no negating adjective that modifies or limits its subject-term, then it ought to be judged *affirmative*: e.g., All citizens are responsible; Some lionesses are tame. But we need also to be alert to the fact that a categorical proposition that has a negated extreme only is most often *affirmative*: e.g., *Not to sin* is laudable; All *nonveterans* are courageous; All veterans are *noncommunicative*; Some *nonveterans* are *nontaxpayers*.

As to the discernment of categorical propositions that are *negative* in quality, there is little or no question when the verb-copula of the proposition is *manifestly negative* in appearance: e.g., Peter is not humane; Some boy scouts are not rugged; All women are not ladylike. But if, when the verb-copula is *apparently positive*, the categorical proposition contains a negating adjective or adverb that directly influences the subject-term and indirectly affects the verb-copula in a nonpositive manner, then it ought to be judged *negative*: e.g., *Not all* wives *are* good cooks; *No* politicians *are* unfair. Obviously, adeptness in distinguishing quickly the logical *quality* of categorical propositions is a definite advantage in the evaluation of arguments.

(b)

Besides possessing a distinctive quality, every categorical or atomic proposition can be put in one of four *quantitative* categories: *singular, indefinite, particular,* or *universal*. This aspect of a categorical proposition is generally dependent on the *extension-factor* or *denotation* of its subject-term: e.g., Some poems are metrical; No human person is omnipotent; Not all Europeans are Italians; Plato is philosophical; Teenagers relish challenges.

The *singular* and *indefinite* categorical propositions are not hard to identify.[3] The *singular* proposition is one in which the subject-term has reference to some individual person or thing: e.g., Jack Ruby made the headlines; Leibniz was a competent logician; That orange is not ripe; This hat is not mine. By comparison, the *indefinite* proposition is one in which there is a great deal of indeterminateness about the subject-term, as suggested by such terms as *any, whoever,* and *whatever*: e.g., Whatever is moved is moved by another; Anything lovable is knowable. As a general rule-of-thumb indefinite categorical propositions are reducible, depending upon the context, to either a *universal* or a *particular* proposition.

Our interest as logicians, however, lies more with the particular and the universal forms of the categorical proposition. The *particular* proposition is the type we most commonly use, yet to identify one is not always easy. In general, a categorical proposition in which the subject-term is limited by such words as *some, not all,* and *not every* is *particular*: e.g., Some roads in California are freeways; Not every soldier is brave; Not all rodents are squirrels.

The *universal* form of the categorical proposition is one whose subject-term includes such quantifiers as *all, every, no,* and *none,* followed always by an *apparently positive* verb-copula: e.g., All stars are bright; Every angel is immaterial; No social worker is selfish; None of the nuns are nervous. In the light of what has been said, the following propositional statements are rightly regarded as *particular* and *not universal*: e.g., All diplomats in the U. N. are not pro-Russian; Not every noncitizen is a nonvoter. Sometimes the validity of universal statements has been seriously challenged, i.e., how can all the objects of a class or set be verified. This challenge can be resolved adequately if the precise meaning of such statements were recognized. For example, the categorical proposition *Every x is y* really asserts that, if an *x* exists actually or potentially, then that *x* possesses an attribute called *y*; whereas the categorical proposition *No x is y* really asserts that there does not exist actually or potentially an individual *x* to which attribute *y* can belong. This meaning of the

universal categorical proposition has a basic affinity to the principle of Universal Instantiation used in modern logic.[4]

Before concluding this functional treatment of the categorical
propositions, we should introduce the student to the *traditional
symbols* which have been used over the centuries as a shorthand
way to indicate the dual aspect of all universal or particular categorical propositions. Like any convention, these symbols are
quite arbitrary in themselves: *A, E, I, O.* The letters *A* and *I*
will be used to signify only affirmative categorical propositions;
the letter *A* will be used to designate those categorical propositions that are *both affirmative and universal*; the letter *I* will be
used to designate those categorical propositions that are *both
affirmative and particular*. The letters *E* and *O* will be used to
signify only negative categorical propositions; the letter *E* will be
used to designate those categorical propositions that are *both
negative and universal*; the letter *O* will be used to designate
those categorical propositions that are *both negative and particular*. These letters were chosen to label these categorical propositions because they are the first two vowels in two Latin words:
AffIrmo (I affirm) and n*EgO* (I deny). In the remainder of this
book we shall employ these symbols in talking about or in identifying forms of categorical propositions.

II

The second general type or class of propositions is the *noncategorical* proposition, also known as the hypothetical or compound
proposition. It is a truth-value statement that signifies *more than
a single intellectual judgment*. In its normal or standardized form,
the noncategorical proposition consists of two or more categorical
propositions joined together by a sentential connective, such as
if then; *either or*: e.g., If (students study), then (they pass their
tests); Either (they like coffee), or (they will remain thirsty).
Unlike the categorical proposition whose principal parts are *term-
extremes*, the noncategorical proposition is principally made up
of *propositional extremes*. Neither is the logical unity of the non-

categorical proposition considered to be as perfect as that of the categorical proposition.[5] These are the chief factors underlying the major differences between categorical and noncategorical propositions which are poles apart in the same logical genus of proposition.

Noncategorical propositions can take many forms, but they have traditionally been classified in a two-fold way: (1) *explicit* and (2) *implicit*.[6] Explicit noncategorical propositions are easily recognizable because their sentential connectives are quite apparent: e.g., If (birds fly), then (birds have wings). There are three common types or species of explicit noncategorical propositions: *conditional, disjunctive,* and *conjunctive*. Implicit noncategorical propositions, on the other hand, do not appear at first to be genuinely noncategorical. This is so because they are actually in disguise, as is easily seen upon analysis, and are for this reason called *exponibles*. They are usually identifiable by their use of such words as *only, except,* and *insofar as*: e.g., Only men have a sense of humor; No students except the freshmen are chow-hounds. There are also three common types or species of implicit noncategorical propositions: *exclusive, exceptive,* and *reduplicative*. Though nearly all such exponibles can ultimately be reduced to one of the standardized forms of the explicit noncategorical proposition, each of the types or species merits some consideration.

(a)

A list of the three types of the *explicit noncategorical* proposition follows, with a brief explanation of each:

(1) *Conditional*—Composed of two or more categorical statements linked together by some form of the sentential connective *if then* (e.g., unless). Its principal parts are known as the *antecedent* and the *consequent*.

The *antecedent* is that which comes before and is generally preceded by the word *if*: e.g., *If* it rains, then the graduation will be held in the gym. The *consequent* is that which follows, or is being inferred or implied, and is generally preceded by the word *then*: e.g., If it rains, *then* the graduation will be held in the gym. However, it is not necessary that the antecedent always have the priority of place in such statements, though it usually does.

Additional examples of the typical conditional proposition are the following: (a) If the Congo's deeply-rooted political problems are solved, then African unity will be more than a dream; (b) Unless you pay the dentist's bill, your credit-reputation will suffer; (c) Had we known you wanted to go to see the hockey game, we would have changed our plans; (d) The Red Sox will win the pennant if, and only if, their pitching continues to improve.

(2) *Disjunctive*—Composed of two or more categorical statements linked together by some form of the sentential connective *either or* (e.g., neither nor). In this type of proposition a choice of alternates is always involved: e.g., Either they will take the serum, or they will not be immunized; The Apollo astronauts could neither get out of the capsule nor extinguish the fire. Ancient logicians were the first to recognize that disjunctive propositions are of two distinct types, the *strong disjunction* and the *weak disjunction*.[7]

The *strong* (or *strict*) disjunctive proposition is one that signifies that the choice is of one and only one of the alternates, because of some basic opposition: e.g., Either Russian ships will be searched, or they will be sunk; You may have either coffee or tea (but not both). The *weak* disjunctive is not as exclusive as to the choices offered, and is by far the more common type of disjunction: e.g., Either you can fly, or you can take a train, or you can walk to Montreal; Lloyd is either going to continue his studies, or join some branch of the military service, or take a trip around the world, or commit suicide.

(3) *Conjunctive*—Sometimes called *copulative*; composed of two or more categorical statements linked together by a sentential connective such as *and*, *moreover*, and *but*: e.g., Jack Kennedy

was assassinated, and Johnson took the oath of Office in the plane; Sugar is sweet, but it is fattening. Logicians are in agreement that every conjunctive proposition has a true truth-value only if its conjuncts (propositional extremes) are all *true*; otherwise it would have a false truth-value. As we shall see in a later chapter, logicians are equally in agreement about the truth-values of the other noncategorical propositions.

(b)

The three types of the *implicit noncategorical* proposition are, as we have seen, *exclusive*, *exceptive*, and *reduplicative*, each of which will now be explained:

(1) *Exclusive*—An exponible that usually contains verbal signifiers such as *only* and *alone*, adverbs indicating some measure of uniqueness or distinctiveness: e.g., (a) Paul is the only veteran in the class; (b) Only Man of all animals manifests a sense of humor; (c) The President alone knows the problem. Each of these propositions can easily be resolved into at least two categorical or atomic statements: e.g., "Only Man of all animals manifests a sense of humor" can be resolved into: Every man has a sense of humor; Nothing else in the animal kingdom has a sense of humor; or, Every thing with a sense of humor is a Man; or even, No man is without a sense of humor.

(2) *Exceptive*—An exponible that usually contains the word *except*, or some similar verbal signifier that suggests a noticeable restriction on the quantification of either its subject-term or its predicate-term: e.g., All students, except the seniors, are irresponsible agents. Propositions of this type are also resolvable into at least two categorical statements: e.g., No senior is an irresponsible agent; All seniors are responsible agents; or, No irresponsible agent is a senior; All seniors are responsible agents. This species of exponible usually can be translated into the conjunctive form of the noncategorical proposition.

(3) *Reduplicative*—An exponible that usually contains such words as *to the extent* and *insofar as*, which signify in a mildly emphatic way the very reason why the subject-term or predicate-term is such and such: e.g., (a) Caesar, insofar as he was a citizen, was eligible for election to that office; (b) Any man, to the extent that he is a plant, can grow; (c) As President, Mr. Johnson deserved to be respected. This species of exponible can usually be translated into the conditional form of the non-categorical proposition.

Further discussion of noncategorical propositions will be purposely postponed to later chapters in which we shall examine the important part they play as premises in the noncategorical or compound syllogism.

III

Our functional consideration of the major types or classes of propositions can be concluded by a brief analysis of the *modal proposition*. Aristotle has been recognized by some scholarly logicians as the *creator* of modal logic, and his investigations into this difficult matter are reputed to be memorable.[8] Still, his treatment of modal logic has met with some reservations from critics; nevertheless, for our purposes he is a sufficiently reliable guide through the common forms of modal propositions.

Modal propositions have a general affinity with the categorical proposition. In this class of proposition the *manner* in which the predicate-term or attribute is related to or unrelated to the subject-term of the same proposition is *explicitly expressed*: e.g., Men are possibly virtuous; Circles are impossibly square. Modal propositions indicate the manner of this relationship, either positive or negative, that can or does obtain between the term-extremes of propositional statements. Mere modifications of the subject-term or of the predicate-term of a truth-value statement are not enough to warrant calling such propositions *modal*: e.g., Peter sings *sweetly*; The just man works *diligently*; The *singing* waitress is efficient. Such modifiers affect only the parts of each proposition, not the mode of their composition.

In the standardized modal proposition, that part has been traditionally called the *dictum* which is the simple assertion that the predicate-term belongs or does not belong to its subject-term; the *mode* factor designates how the term-extremes of the proposition are united or separated: e.g., It is impossible that any man is not an animal. The *mode* is signified by the phrase it is *impossible*; the *dictum* is the statement *any man is not an animal*. The logician is chiefly interested in the modal feature of these propositions because the nature of things, other than second intentions, is not of much relevance to him as a logician. Modal propositions are expressed in four general ways: *possibility*, *impossibility*, *contingency*, and *necessity*. Each of these modes will now be analyzed:

(1) *Possibility* is expressed in a modal proposition to signify that something has the capacity to do or not to do something, or that something has some natural disposition to receive something. Generally, this type of proposition states simply that there is *no inherent contradiction* for something to act along certain lines or to be so acted upon: e.g., (a) It is possible that men will reach the moon; (b) It is not possible that a circle will ever be squared; (c) It is possible that high-schoolers can learn logic.

(2) *Impossibility* is expressed in a modal proposition to signify that there exists *some inherent incompatibility* in something either to do or to suffer a certain thing: e.g., (a) It is impossible that any water be dry; (b) It is impossible that angels are corporeal; (c) It is not impossible that jailbirds write poetry.

(3) *Contingency* is expressed in a modal proposition to signify that something can be this way or that way without any essential change in the entity itself: e.g., (a) It is contingent that some women are wealthy; (b) Men are contingently virtuous; (c) It is not contingent that men die.

(4) *Necessity* is expressed in a modal proposition to signify that something is not able to have itself other than it essentially is:[9] e.g., (a) All animals are necessarily corruptible; (b) That

men be corporeal is necessary; (c) It is not necessary that all men are white; (d) To cross the Atlantic Ocean by plane is not absolutely necessary.

Before concluding this analysis of the modal proposition, we should note that there are norms for judging correctly both the quality and quantity of such propositions. The *quality* of any modal proposition hinges only on the positive or negative way the modality is designated: e.g., "It *is* impossible that all angels are saints" is an *affirmative* proposition: "It *is not* necessary that all men attain salvation" is a *negative* proposition. Generally, as to their *quantity*, necessary and impossible modal propositions are considered to be *universal*; possible and contingent modal propositions are considered to be *particular*. In the next chapter, the salient properties of categorical propositions will be studied.

Pertinent Quotations about the kinds of propositions:

(a)

The first class of simple propositions is the simple affirmation, the next, the simple denial; all others are only one by conjunction. Every proposition must contain a verb or the tense of a verb. The phrase which defines the species *man*, if no verb in present, past, or future time be added, is not a proposition. It may be asked how the expression *a footed animal with two feet* can be called single; for it is not the circumstance that the words follow in unbroken succession that effects the unity. This inquiry, however, finds its place in an investigation foreign to that before us.

We call those propositions single which indicate a single fact, or the conjunction of the parts of which results in unity: those propositions, on the other hand, are separate and many in number, which indicate many facts, or whose parts have no conjunction.

> —*The Basic Works of Aristotle*, tr. R. McKeon (New York: Random House, 1941), "On Interpretation," p. 42; by permission of the Clarendon Press, Oxford.

(b)

Indeed there is another sub-division of proposition: if the proposition is simple (*una*), it is either affirmative or negative. Moreover, the affirmative proposition has a priority over the negative proposition because of three factors mentioned earlier, where it was said that the word is the symbol of the concept and the concept is the symbol of the thing. Therefore, on the part of the *word* (*vox*), the affirmative proposition has a priority of simplicity over the negative proposition because the negative proposition adds a particular negative to the affirmative. Likewise, on the part of the *concept*, because the affirmative proposition signifies a composition of ideas, whereas the negative proposition signifies their division; for division is naturally posterior to composition. And just as there is no corruption of things unless they exist, so there is no division of things unless they are composites. The priority of existence of the *thing* over its nonexistence is another reason why the affirmative proposition precedes the negative proposition, just as anything possessed by the very nature of the thing is prior to its loss.

—St. Thomas Aquinas, *Commentary on Aristotle's On Interpretation*, lesson 8 (author's translation).

(c)

Every proposition either affirms something of something, e.g., *Zayd is wise, Zayd stands*, or negates something of something, e.g., *Zayd does not stand*. That proposition which affirms something of something, we call an affirmative proposition; that which negates something of something, we call a negative proposition.

The affirmative proposition may affirm the predicate of all the subject, e.g., *Every man is an animal*; and we call it a universal affirmative, and we call *every* a universal affirmative sign. It may affirm the predicate of a part of the subject, e.g., *Some men write*; and this we call a particular affirmative, and we call *some* a particular affirmative sign. The negative proposition may negate the predicate of all of the subject, e.g., *No man is a stone*; and this we call a universal negative, and we call *no* a universal negative sign. It may negate the predicate of a part of the subject, e.g., *Not every man writes*, or *Some men do not write*, or *Not some men write*; and this we call a particular negative. We do not discriminate among these three expressions of the particular negative; nevertheless, we always prefer our expression in the particular negative to be *not every*, which we call the particular negative sign. The signs then are four: *every, some, no*, and *not every*: universal affirmative, particular affirmative, universal negative, and particular negative.

> —Moses Maimonides' *Treatise on Logic*, chap. 2, by I. Efros, as appeared in Roland Houde's *Readings in Logic* (Dubuque: W. C. Brown Co., 1958), pp. 181–182.

(d)

An exponible proposition is one whose meaning is obscure and requires an exposition because of some syncategorematic (word) implicitly or explicitly contained in it, or contained in some word, as in the following: *Man only is animal, Sortes begins to be white, The line is infinite*, and so on. In cases of this kind it must be noted that those things responsible for a proposition being exponible differ in many ways. For some are exclusive signs, as *only, alone*; others are exceptive, as *with the exception of, but* (nisi); some are reduplicative, as *insofar as, according as*; others introduce beginning or ending, as *begins, ends*; others introduce privation of end, as *infinite*; others introduce excess, as adjectives in the comparative and the superlative degree; others introduce a distinction, as *differs, other than*, and so on; others introduce a special mode of distribution, as *whole, any one you please*, and so on. On account of these (syncategorematic words) the proposition becomes obscure and requires exposition, and so they are said to make a proposition exponible.

> —Peter of Spain (Pope John XXI), *Summulae Logicales*, tract VII, treatise "On Exponibles," tr. and edit. by Joseph P. Mullally (Notre Dame, Indiana: University of Notre Dame Press, 1960), p. 105.

(e)

I answer that, true affirmative propositions can be formed about God. To prove this we must know that in every true affirmative proposition the predicate and the subject signify in some way the same thing in reality, and different things in idea. And this appears to be the case both in propositions which have an accidental predicate, and in those which have an essential predicate. For it is manifest that *man* and *white* are the same in subject, and different in idea; for the idea of man is one thing, and that of whiteness is another. The same applies when I say, *man is an animal*; since the same thing which is man is truly animal; for in the same *suppositum* there is sensible nature by reason of which he is called animal, and the rational nature by reason of which he is called man; hence here again predicate and subject are the same as to *suppositum,* but different as to idea. But in propositions where one same thing is predicated of itself, the same rule in some way applies, inasmuch as the intellect draws to the *suppositum* what it places in the subject; and what it places in the predicate it draws to the nature of the form existing in the *suppositum*; according to the saying that *predicates are to be taken formally, and subjects materially.* To this diversity in idea corresponds the plurality of predicate and subject, while the intellect signifies the identity of the thing by the composition itself.

—St. Thomas Aquinas, *Summa Theologica*, part I, quest. 13, art. 12, tr. Fathers of the English Dominican Province (New York: Benziger Bros., 1947), vol. I, p. 71.

Exercise:

In the spaces provided before each propositional statement, identify it as simple (categorical) or compound (noncategorical); if *categorical*, using the traditional symbols (*A-E-I-O*), indicate its quantity and quality; if *noncategorical*, identify it as exactly as possible.

(1) .... No Africans are Communists.

(2) .... Castro will either remain a Red pawn or capitulate to the U. N.

(3) .... All nonunionists are not bakers.

(4) .... Only seniors will apply for jobs this spring.

(5) .... Not all sailors will be tattooed.

(6) .... Spiders, inasmuch as they are insects, are irritating.

(7) .... Every general in the NATO forces is not American.

(8) .... If you invest your earnings in IBM stock, you'll make money.

(9) .... The Red Sox will win the pennant, and they will be victorious in the World Series.

(10) .... Except for Al Kaline, the Detroit Tigers aren't strong batters.

(11) .... No man can serve two masters.

(12) .... Not every college student is a hippie.

(13) .... No socialists are nonpacifists.

(14) . . . . It is not possible that Christ is a human person.

(15) . . . . That rocks are substances is necessary.

(16) . . . . God alone is omnipotent.

(17) . . . . There are only five predicables.

(18) . . . . Some American-made cars are over-priced.

(19) . . . . All imperialists are not British.

(20) . . . . The Berlin Wall is an ominous reality.

(21) . . . . Not all golfers are experts.

(22) . . . . Some skiers are sexagenarians.

(23) . . . . It is contingent that New England is so verdant.

(24) . . . . It is not impossible that everything is not absolute.

(25) . . . . No college professors are omniscient.

6

Properties of the Categorical Proposition

Besides being able to signify, the standardized categorical proposition is often the source of *implications* or of *inferences*. Up to this point we have studied the signification and structure of propositions in their isolated condition as logical units. But propositions are not just units or ends in themselves; they are likewise the parts of which simple and complex arguments are composed. It is time now to conclude our consideration of the many dimensions of the proposition, as such, and to begin examining some of the *elementary* forms of argumentation.

Rudimentary forms of rational discourse are based on *immediate inferences*; such forms have been known traditionally as the *properties* of the categorical proposition. Inference or implication is simply the process of "drawing out" other statements from a proposition or a set of propositions: for example, the assertion "All x are y" ordinarily implies that the statement "Some x are not y" would have a *false* truth-value; so also, (if) "no x is y," (and if) "all z is y," (then) one could *validly infer* that "no z is x." In other words, the ability to see inferences of any kind is a sign of a developed power of perceiving logical relationships.

Inferences can be either *mediate* or *immediate*. As illustrated in the second example in the previous paragraph, the *mediate* inference is evidently quite complex and structured along the rigorous lines of formal argumentation. Generally a mediate inference involves a pair of propositions (premises) that have some common middle-term. In subsequent chapters we will study the major forms of argumentation in which mediate inference plays a prominent part. Our present concern, however, is more with *immediate* inferences which are naturally far less complex and far more spontaneous: for example, the categorical proposition "No x is y" ordinarily implies that the statement "some x are y" has a false truth-value. No other proposition need be tacitly assumed (as we shall see is necessary in what is called an *enthymeme*)[1] to make such an implication. Of course, only valid inferences are consistent with the basic laws of correct reasoning.

Immediate inferences come easily and naturally to most men. It is an inclination as innate to us as our desire to know and to communicate with each other. Experience testifies that from our earliest years we are prone to make inferences. When a youngster hears the statement "All married men are not happy," he may quite naturally infer "my barber may be married" if he sees him always with a scowl on his face. In almost every branch of systematic knowledge, logical inferences of the immediate type come into prominent play. Not infrequently in such areas as economics and engineering such inferences are helpful in predicting phenomena not yet actually observed.

But despite man's propensity to draw out implications, not all of these inferences are logically correct. They are logically incorrect because they do not satisfy the conditions for valid inference. Experience often awakens us to our tendency to be fallible in such acts of inferring, for fallacious inferences are by no means a rarity. In order to understand why this should be so and how it can be eliminated to some extent, one must know the various types of *immediate inference* and the approved rules that can ensure their logical validity. Given this knowledge, one can then proceed with confidence to a study of more formalized argumentation in subsequent chapters.

In the following analysis of the more important *properties* of the categorical proposition, we shall proceed on the general assumption, as did Aristotle in his interpretation of them, that all the classes of entities employed in our illustrations have *real members*. In this way the demands concerning *existential import* (that they are real existents) will be adequately satisfied; and the attempts of some modern logicians to reject or to ridicule Aristotle's interpretation will be neutralized.[2]

From the categorical proposition, insofar as it is considered a total entity, the following immediate inferences or properties can come about especially in four ways: (1) by *opposition*; (2) by *obversion*; (3) by *conversion*; and (4) by *contraposition*.[3] Each of these major properties will now be examined.

I

Opposition signifies generally a lack of identity that can exist or does exist between entities. In less technical language, we might say that an *immediate inference by opposition* suggests some form of repugnance, some type of hostility, between things; it infers that one thing is not something else, that one thing is different from another thing. Applying this notion to the categorical proposition, Aristotle states that "every affirmation has an opposite denial, and similarly every denial an opposite affirmation."[4]

Opposition between categorical propositions, whether actual or possible, is rooted primarily in differing qualitative factors, secondarily in differing truth-values. An affirmative proposition is *qualitatively opposed* to a negative proposition; truth and falsity are *opposed truth-values*. We need add only the provision that genuinely opposed categorical propositions should have their respective subject-terms and predicate-terms designating and denoting the same entities: e.g., Every man is musical; No man is musical; Not every man is musical. Unless there is this identity of both signification and supposition between the terms of the categorical statements involved, there is no basis for logical opposition between them. There is, for example, no logical opposition in the following sets of propositions:

Peter is *talkative*; Peter is not *athletic*.

Some *teachers* are comical; Some *cooks* are not comical.

All *men* are *musical*; No *zebras* are *slow*.

Nor can the following sets of sub-contrary categorical propositions be said strictly to be logically opposed:

Some citizens are just; Some citizens are not just.

Not every x is y; Some x are y.

In so many instances the reference of the quantifier *some,* or its
equivalent, either is not identical or is ambiguous. Thomas
Aquinas explained why this could be so: ". . . . the subject of
the particular proposition is the universal taken particularly, not
for any determinate individuals, but indeterminately for anyone
at all; and so, when anything about the universal taken particularly is affirmed or denied, that mode of asserting is not had
which is the affirmation and negation of the same subject that is
required for opposition of affirmation and negation, as indicated
previously."[5]

In the strict sense, then, genuine logical opposition as a major
property of the categorical proposition can exist only between
contradictory propositions and between *contrary* propositions.
Examples of *contradictory* opposition would be "All men are
musical," "All men are not musical"; "No x are y," "Some x are
y"; "Peter is musical," "Peter is not musical." In passing it might
be noted that singular propositions are uniquely contradictory.
Examples of *contrary* opposition would be "All men are musical,"
"No men are musical"; "No x are y," "All x are y." It should be
observed that ordinarily only in contradictory opposition of
propositions is there both a qualitative and a quantitative
difference.

Up to this point in our study of the logical opposition of
categorical propositions, emphasis has been placed on what is
traditionally called its *material* phase. But this is not the only

factor of this logical property. There is another aspect of logical opposition that is in some ways more important, viz, the *formal* phase. The formal factor of logical opposition is intimately linked with the *truth-value* of those categorical propositions that are opposed in any way at all. With respect to the truth-value aspect, categorical propositions can be opposed in four ways: (a) as *contradictories*; (b) as *contraries*; (c) as *sub-contraries*; (d) as *subalternates*. The truth-value factor in each type of opposition will be analyzed separately and then schematized at the end of the section with the help of the classical diagram known as the *square of opposition*.

(a) *Contradictory* opposition is the most extreme type of opposition between propositions considered in their formal aspect. Why this is so may be puzzling to many people, perhaps because they have never observed the actual direction most of their arguments are wont to take. The first reaction of many people caught up in argument is to "fight fire with fire." "All Irish-Americans are drunks," says one; "No Irish-Americans are drunks," says another. Or, "No civil-righters are sincere"; "All civil-righters are sincere." In such dialogues more heat is generated than light. As noted earlier, contradictory statements are formulated as categorical propositions that differ both in quality and quantity: e.g., All men are musical, Some men are not musical; No men are musical, Some men are musical.

The core of this type of logical opposition is the manifest incompatibility in truth-value between the propositions. In this most radical form of logical opposition, the particular statement directly attacks the "universality" of the universal proposition's truth-value. In such instances *particular* propositions have a strong neutralizing effect on the wide-sweeping universal assertions. The *particular negative* proposition, for example, denies absolutely and completely what has been stated by the whole proposition that is, taken as a unit, *universally affirmative* (e.g., All men are kind—Some men are not kind; Every sailor is immoral—Not every sailor is immoral).

Similarly, the *particular affirmative* proposition renders totally impotent what has been asserted by the whole proposition that is, taken as a unit, *universally negative* (e.g., No men are musical— Some men are musical; Nothing is absolute—Something is absolute). In contradictory statements no middle-ground remains. As a result, contradictory propositions can simultaneously be neither true nor false as to their truth-value. For example, if the categorical proposition "All men are musical" has a *true truth-value*, then the categorical proposition "Not all men are musical" must have a *false truth-value*. Conversely, if the categorical proposition "No men are musical" has a *false truth-value*, then the categorical proposition "Some men are musical" must have a *true truth-value*. In short, contradictory propositions, taken as units, are diametrically opposed to each other in truth-value. What this analysis makes clear, of course, is the need to avoid making sweeping universal statements of any logical quality unless there is objective evidence to support them.

(b) *Contrary* opposition is the second most extreme type of opposition between categorical propositions. As noted earlier, contrary propositions are alike in their universality of quantification and specifically different in their qualitative factor: e.g., All men are musical; No men are musical. Contrary propositions are fundamentally opposed only in their quality and in their truth-value. In short, they can never simultaneously have a *true truth-value*; but they can simultaneously have a *false truth-value*: e.g., "All Irish-Americans are drunks"; "No Irish-Americans are drunks." Concretely this means that if one proposition has a true truth-value, then its contrary must have a false truth-value. But the converse of this principle does not obtain necessarily and always; that is, if one of the contrary propositions is given as having a false truth-value, it does not necessarily follow that the other proposition must have a true truth-value. In contingent matter both contrary propositions may in fact be false as indicated above. For example, if it is false that "Every actor is amoral" it is not necessarily true that "No actor is amoral"; and likewise, if

"All teachers are patient" is false, "No teachers are patient" is not therefore true.

(c) *Sub-contrary* opposition can exist solely between particular categorical propositions different only in quality and in falsity: i.e., if particular propositions are so opposed, they cannot simultaneously have false truth-values. Hence if one such proposition has a *false truth-value*, then the other will usually have a *true truth-value*. But the converse is not necessarily so, because sometimes in contingent matter both opposed propositions may have a true truth-value (e.g., Some men are lovers; Some men are not lovers). As we observed earlier in this chapter, the quantifier "some" in such opposed categorical propositions frequently does not refer to the same individuals in the set or class. Hence sub-contrary opposition is not a genuine type of logical opposition.

(d) *Subalternate* opposition is also called opposition in a very loose sense, for it never involves categorical propositions with a different qualitative factor. Subalternate propositions differ only in quantity: e.g., All men are musical, Some men are musical; No men are musical, Not all men are musical. From the rules of inference for contradictory and contrary opposition, we can derive some definite norms of validity for all categorical propositions involved in subalternation. If the universal proposition has a true truth-value, then its particular proposition (subaltern) will also have a true truth-value: e.g., if the statement "All men are musical" has a *true* truth-value, then the statement "Some men are musical" also has a *true* truth-value. In subalternation, truth is said to "descend." However, if the particular proposition has a *false* truth-value, then its universal proposition (superaltern) will also have a *false* truth-value: e.g., if the statement "Some men are not musical" has a false truth-value, then the statement "No men are musical" also has a false truth-value. In subalternation, falsity is said to "ascend." The *Square of Opposition* has been for centuries a useful device to illustrate all the truth-values involved in categorical propositions logically opposed, both strictly and loosely.[6]

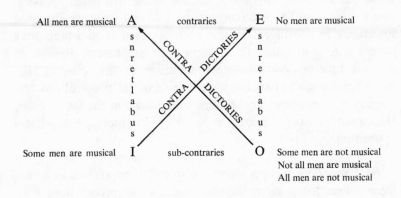

SQUARE OF OPPOSITION

All men are musical **A**   contraries   **E** No men are musical

Some men are musical **I**   sub-contraries   **O** Some men are not musical
Not all men are musical
All men are not musical

II

Obversion involves a categorical proposition inferred immediately from another by denying the opposite of that which the original statement affirms: e.g., "All x is y" validly obverts to "No x is non-y." Traditionally this property of the categorical proposition was also called *equivalence* because the original statement and the statement derived by obversion from it should be *identical in meaning*. In appearance, obversion resembles logical opposition; actually, however, an obversion is simply another special way of saying the same thing. It has some analogy with such arithmetical formulas as $2 + 2 = 4$ and $5 - 1 = 4$. Looked at technically, *obversion* is a logical property that enables two categorical propositions which are qualitatively opposed to possess the same meaning and truth-value.

Obversion is achieved in *two* steps: (1) the *quality* of the "obvertend" (the original proposition) is changed; and (2) *non-* or some other suitable negative particle (e.g., *un-*; *in-*; *im-*) is added as a prefix to the predicate-term of the obvertend: e.g., "All x are y" validly obverts in two steps to "No x are non-y"; and "No nonveterans are patriotic" validly obverts in two steps to "All nonveterans are non-patriotic" or "All nonveterans are nonpatriotic." The quantification factor of the original proposition is never altered in a valid obversion. The proposition formed by obversion is called the "obverse" of the obvertend.

It may seem paradoxical that such a radical mutation in the logical structure of the original categorical proposition does not bring about a substantive change in the meaning and in the truth-value of the obverse. Nevertheless, logicians are quite agreed that in valid obversions neither the meaning nor the truth-value of the obvertend is altered, principally because the particle *non-* prefixed to the predicate-term cancels out or neutralizes the change in the *qualitive* factor of the original proposition: e.g., the statement "*No* non-x is non-y" validly obverts to "*Every* non-x is non-non-y" or "*Every* non-x is y." A few words of caution may prudently be added here, however; in English, many prefixes, such as *in-* and *un-* are not always negative in their signification (e.g., *im*portant, *in*tentional, *un*scramble, *un*wrap). Whenever one is in doubt, he can safely employ the technical prefix *non-* in his obversions.

The *formal* phase of obversion is quite important. If obversion is to be valid, then the *truth-value* of the obvertend and the obverse should be absolutely the same. It can be stated axiomatically that, if the obvertend has a *true* truth-value, then after valid obversion takes place the obverse must also have a *true* truth-value; similarly, if the obvertend has a *false* truth-value, then after valid obversion takes place the obverse must also have a *false* truth value. These next examples of valid obversions may be found helpful in the understanding of this logical property of the categorical proposition: All non-x is y = No non-x is non-y; Some non-x is y = Some non-x is not non-y; No non-x is y = Every non-x is non-y; Not every non-x is y = Some non-x is non-y.

III

Conversion is the third major property of the categorical proposition that we intend to examine. It is really nothing other than a logical process in which the subject-term and the predicate-term of a given categorical proposition are interchanged. However, not all categorical propositions are validly convertible; neither are they all validly converted in the same way. The *O* proposition is not validly convertible, for many reasons. The property of convertibility belongs only to categorical propositions of the *A, E,* and *I* types. *E* and *I* propositions convert *simply*: e.g., "No x is y" validly converts to "No y is x"; and "Some x are y" validly converts to "Some y are x." Sometimes the *A* proposition also converts in this manner, as in a perfect definitory statement (e.g., All men are risible beings; All risible beings are men); but in its normal or standardized form the *A* proposition is wont to be converted *accidentally*: e.g., "All men are animals" validly converts to "Some animals are men." Since the validity of the converting process is based on what is called *distribution,* this logical notion must now be analyzed.

Distribution is a logical notion that is intimately tied up with the *quantification* factor of both the subject-term and the predicate-term of the categorical propositions involved in conversion, i.e., the convertend and the converse. *Quantification* is a notion closely associated with the extensionality or the range of a term as it is employed in such propositions. In logic, the extensionality of any such term or common name simply indicates or denotes the number of individual members to which that term or common name has some reference. In other words, the notion of extension signifies the quantity of things commonly sharing a special kind of being. Sometimes the reference is singularized (e.g., Paulinus is philosophical); in most cases, however, the reference is pluralized (e.g., All monkeys are mammals; Some freshmen are athletic; Not every housewife is a homemaker; Whoever does not diet, dies).

A logician's interpretation of quantification in relation to the extremes of a categorical proposition is inevitably influenced by his theory of predication. For Aristotle and his followers, the *extension* of any subject-term or predicate-term in a categorical proposition is rooted in and formally dependent upon its *comprehension* or *comprehensibility*, i.e., the natural perfections that necessarily go into the composition of an entity; for anything is knowable to the extent that it is perfect, and is perfect insofar as it is actual. In other words, things exist individually prior to our knowledge of their existence as a class by which they can subsequently be denoted in propositional statements. The comprehensibility and extensionality of a term always vary inversely; i.e., the more of the one, the less of the other (e.g., All horses are animals; All lions are animals). Nominalists and Positivists tend to differ sharply with Aristotle and his followers in this area of logic.

Any subject-term or predicate-term is said to be *distributed* only when that term is taken in its pure and total universality, i.e., when it refers to each and every member of that designated class or species without exception. It can be either all-inclusive or all-exclusive: e.g., *All x* are y; *No x* are y. The subject-term of every universal categorical proposition (*A*, *E*) is distributed, regardless of the qualitative factor. The predicate-term of every negative categorical proposition (*E*, *O*) is likewise distributed, regardless of the quantitative factor. This is so because of the divisive nature of the absolute denial expressed by the negative categorical proposition (e.g., No traitors are patriotic; Not all men are penurious; All women are not immoral; Some lions are not tame). Over the distributed extreme in a categorical proposition it is customary, for purposes of analysis, to write the capital letter *D*:

D   D
No men are rocks.

D
Some men are not polite.

D
Not every dog is a thoroughbred.

On the other hand, any common term employed in the extremes of a categorical proposition is said to be *undistributed* if and only if it refers to a part or section of the members of the class or species designated by that term: e.g., *Some men* are heroic; *Not every lioness* is ferocious; All sparrows are *birds*; Some fish are *dolphins*. In the concrete, then, the subject-term of every particular categorical proposition (*I, O*) is *undistributed*, regardless of its qualitative factor (e.g., Not every x is y; Some x is z); and the predicate-term of every affirmative categorical proposition (*A, I*)—except perfect definitory statements, which are symmetrically identical as noted earlier—likewise is undistributed, regardless of its quantitative factor (e.g., All senators are *citizens*; Some martyrs were *Romans*).

That the *particular* categorical proposition (*I, O*) ought to have an *undistributed* subject-term may not be difficult to understand. But it is not so easy for one to understand why the predicate-term of the *affirmative* categorical proposition ought to be *undistributed*. It is so because the common name or term employed as the predicate-term of the standardized affirmative categorical proposition is evidently and really much broader and more inclusive in its extensionality than its subject-term; as a result, it is used only in a *partial and limited sense*. In short, the predicate-term of an affirmative categorical proposition is not totally exhausted by the subject-term, is not totally extended as to its universality, except as noted earlier. Over the undistributed extreme in a categorical proposition it is customary, for the purposes of analysis, to write the capital letter *U*:

$$U \qquad U$$
Some cows are brownish.

$$D \qquad U$$
All men are animals.

$$U \qquad D$$
Not every dog is tall.

Historically, the difficulty of discerning the quantification of the extremes of categorical propositions has been constantly recognized even as far back as the ancient logicians. Over the centuries, in order to aid the student, ingenious methods of illustrating class relations in categorical propositions, by themselves and in arguments, have emphasized the use of geometrical figures; the efforts of Leibniz, Euler, and Venn in this area are most popular (see footnote 6). Below is a simple schema intended as an aid to memory; it also shows clearly when the extremes in categorical propositions are *distributed* (D), when *undistributed* (U), and when *indefinite* (x):

Proposition	Subject-term	Predicate-term
A & E	D	x
E & O	x	D
I & O	U	x
A & I	x	U

Having seen what is meant by the notion of *distribution* in logic, we should now be better conditioned to proceed to inquire WHY some categorical propositions are *simply convertible,* and some are not. Only the *E* and the *I* propositions are simply convertible; *A* propositions normally are only accidentally convertible; *O* propositions are never convertible validly. The logical reasons for the convertibility or nonconvertibility of categorical propositions are not too difficult to understand provided one remembers that in any valid conversion neither the quality nor the truth-value of the convertend (the original proposition) may be altered.

(a) *Simple* conversion (*E* and *I*) merely involves an interchange of the extremes of a categorical proposition without altering its quantitative and qualitative features or its truth-value. It can be validly done only because some categorical propositions are so structured that there exists an equity or identity of distribution between subject-term and predicate-term. The standardized universal negative, *E*, and the standardized particular affirmative, *I*, are such categorical propositions. In the *E* proposition both extremes are distributed. Therefore, every *E* proposition can be simply converted validly:

> No men are angels. (Convertend)
>
> No angels are men. (Converse)
>
> None of the ball players took a bribe. (Convertend)
>
> No takers of a bribe were ball players. (Converse)

On the other hand, in the *I* proposition both extremes are undistributed. Therefore, every *I* proposition can likewise be simply converted validly:

> Some Americans are disloyal to their country. (Convertend)
>
> Some people disloyal to their country are Americans. (Converse)

Still another way of showing the reasonableness of simple conversion is to attempt an opposition between relevant categorical propositions: if the proposition "Some Americans are Communists" has a given *true* truth-value, then its converse "Some Communists are Americans" will also have a true truth-value, because of the validity of simple conversion. Otherwise, the propositional statement "Some Americans are Communists" would have contradictory truth-values simultaneously: for, if (a) "Some Americans are Communists" (convertend) is true, then (b) "Some Communists are Americans" (converse) is likewise true; hence (c) "No Communists are Americans" (contradiction) is false, and (d) "No Americans are Communists" (valid converse of *c*) is also false; while (e) "Some Americans are Communists" (contradiction of *d*) is then true. But, if (a) "Some Americans are Communists" (convertend) is given as *true*, then (b) "Some Communists are Americans" (converse of *a*) should be likewise true; however, if it had been made false in the process of simple conversion then (c) "No Communists are Americans," its contradictory, would have a true truth-value, and

(d) "No Americans are Communists," its valid converse, would also have a true truth-value; hence (e) "Some Americans are Communists," the contradictory of *c*, would then have a *false* truth-value. But this is logically impossible because the original statement, "Some Americans are Communists," was given as *true*.

(b) *Accidental* conversion (*A*) is a valid logical procedure but is imperfect and limited because it does involve a quantitative change in the converse.[7] Still it is the only way possible to convert validly the standardized *A* proposition which has an inequity of distribution between its extremes that are to be interchanged. In the *A* proposition, the subject-term is distributed and the predicate-term is undistributed. Therefore, the *A* proposition validly converts only accidentally. In short, to infer that "All animals are men" from the original statement that "All men are animals" is both invalid and false. In order to preserve the basic meaning of the standardized *A* proposition, neither its qualitative factor nor its truth-value can be altered. Conversion of the *A* proposition, then, can be validly achieved only if its predicate-term remains undistributed in the interchanging process. The distributive character of the subject-term will necessarily suffer some diminution in the procedure but there will be no formal or substantial loss of its original meaning or truth-value:

$$D \qquad U$$
All cats are (some) animals.

$$U \qquad U$$
Some animals are cats.

Another way of showing the reasonableness of this type of valid conversion involving the standardized *A* proposition is to attempt an opposition between relevant categorical propositions: if the convertend "All cats are animals" has a given *true* truth-value, then its converse "Some animals are cats" will also have a true truth-value, because of the validity of accidental conversion. But if this were not so and the statement "Some animals are cats" were to have a false truth-value, then "No animals are cats," its contradictory, would have to have a true truth-value. In turn, its valid converse, "No cats are animals," would likewise have a true truth-value; but, then, this situation would lead to contraries, "No cats are animals" and "All cats are animals," being simultaneously true which is inconsistent with the basic laws of correct reasoning.

(c) The *O* proposition is *never validly convertible*. This is due almost exclusively to the combination of two factors about the particular negative: its quality and the inequity of distribution of its extremes. If the subject-term, which is undistributed, is to be interchanged with the predicate-term of the *O* proposition, then immediately it would usurp an extension greater than it originally possessed; for every negative categorical proposition has a distributed predicate-term. From such a logically invalid procedure, coupled with the divisive tendency inherent in the negative type of statement, the *truth-value* of the convertend would have to be tampered with substantially. The closest any negative particular proposition can come to being changed validly in a radical way is by means of *contraposition*, which is the logical property we must now take up.

IV

Contraposition can be validly achieved only with *A* and *O* categorical propositions. As a kind of immediate inference, it is a lot like a cocktail (e.g., a Martini or a Manhattan) insofar as it is a smooth blending of some of the logical properties of the categorical proposition. Actually contraposition consists of one unit of "conversion" and two units of "obversion": (i) the original proposition is validly obverted: (ii) the obverse resulting is then validly converted; and (iii) the resulting converse is then validly obverted. Another simpler way of achieving the same final result is merely to add the prefix *non-* to each of the extremes of the *A* and *O* categorical propositions and then to interchange the extremes. "All x are y" is validly contraposed to "All non-y are non-x"; and "Not all Africans are blacks" is validly contraposed to "Not all non-blacks are non-Africans." In valid contraposing, the original meaning of the categorical proposition will be preserved provided its quality, quantity, and truth-value are not specifically changed. However, neither the *E* nor the *I* types of categorical proposition can be validly contraposed, because inevitably some logical law of inference would be violated in the process. The *E* proposition cannot be validly contraposed because its quantitative factor would be altered substantially in the second step of the process: e.g.,

> *Original:* No x is y.
>
> *Obverse:* All x is non-y. (First step)
>
> *Converse:* Some non-y is x. (Second Step)
>
> *Obverse:* Some non-y is not non-x. (Third step)

The *I* proposition likewise cannot be validly contraposed because the second step results in an *O* proposition, and as we learned earlier in the chapter no *O* proposition is validly convertible: e.g.,

> *Original:* Some x is y.
>
> *Obverse:* Some x is not non-y. (First step)
>
> *Converse:* invalid; "Some non-y is not x" would result, but then the term *x* has taken on an extension greater than it had before conversion.

Pertinent Quotations about the salient properties of categorical propositions:

(a)

Distribution is the multiplication of a common term achieved through a universal sign, as when it is said, *Every man is running.* The term *man* is distributed or is spread out to each and every one of its inferiors through this sign *every*, and so there is a kind of multiplication. Moreover, I say *of a common term*, because the singular term is not able to be *distributed*. Whence these expressions are incongruous: Every Socrates; Every Plato; and any other similar ones.

> —Peter of Spain (Pope John XXI), *Summulae Logicales*, bk. VII, tract XII (author's translation).

(b)

But truly in contradictions the negation is so pure and absolute that it destroys every agreement with its own extreme denial, and so there remains neither being, nor aptitude, nor universality, nor particularity, for it cuts off, as it were, the totality of a malignant nature. Whence, simply and absolutely, this opposition is intensively greater, and from it is derived other forms of opposition as from the prime analogate. And to the extent they can lay claim to be opposed, they will be, commensurate with the sharing they have in contradiction.

> —John of St. Thomas, *ibid.*, part I, Illus., quest. 7, art. 1 (author's translation).

(c)

Since the contrary of the proposition *every animal is just* is *no animal is just*, it is plain that these two propositions will never both be true at the same time or with reference to the same subject. Sometimes, however, the contradictories of these contraries will both be true, as in the instance before us: the propositions *not every animal is just* and *some animals are just* are both true.

Further, the proposition *no man is just* follows from the proposition *every man is non-just*; and the proposition *not every man is non-just*, which is the opposite of *every man is non-just*, follows from the proposition *some men are just*; for if this be true, there must be some just men.

> —*The Basic Works of Aristotle*, tr. R. McKeon (New York: Random House, 1941), "On Interpretation," ch. 10, p. 51; by permission of the Clarendon Press, Oxford.

(d)

Conversion is a mutation of the extremes of a proposition, from the subject to the predicate and from the predicate to the subject, but with its quality and truth remaining the same.

> —John of St. Thomas, *ibid.,* bk. 2, ch. 19 (author's translation).

(e)

Equivalence is a certain convertibility of propositions which results from the ordination of this adverb *non* having been placed before contradictories and after contraries and both for subalterns with universal and particular signs. Equivalence is two-fold: simple and compound. Simple is exemplified in those words, as risible is convertible with man, and this is called *simple inherence.* . . . Conversion through *contraposition* is to make the predicate from the subject and the subject from the predicate by changing from definite to indefinite terms, yet preserving the quality and quantity of the original proposition; and in this way the universal affirmative is changed into itself and the particular negative also, as *Every man is an animal* becomes *Every non-animal is a non-man.*

> —Peter of Spain (Pope John XXI), *Summulae Logicales,* bk. VII, tract I (author's translation).

(f)

An affirmation is opposed to a denial in the sense which I denote by the term *contradictory,* when, while the subject remains the same, the affirmation is of universal character and the denial is not. The affirmation *every man is white* is the *contradictory* of the denial, *not every man is white;* or again, the proposition *no man is white* is the *contradictory* of the proposition *some men are white.* But propositions are opposed as *contraries* when both the affirmation and the denial are universal, as in the sentences *every man is white, no man is white; every man is just, no man is just.*

We see that in a pair of this sort both propositions cannot be true, but the contradictories of a pair of contraries can sometimes both be true with reference to the same subject; for instance, *not every man is white* and *some men are white* are both true. Of such corresponding positive and negative propositions as refer to universals and have a universal character, one must be true and the other false. This is the case also when the reference is to individuals, as in the propositions *Socrates is white, Socrates is not white*.

—*The Basic Works of Aristotle*, tr. R. McKeon (New York: Random House, 1941), "On Interpretation," ch. 7, p. 44; by permission of the Clarendon Press, Oxford.

Exercises:

I. *Opposition*

A. In the spaces provided, write out what is requested:

(1) *Contrary* of *All sailors are brave*:

(2) *Subaltern* of *No politicians are rogues*:

(3) *Contradictory* of *All scientists are lovers*:

(4) *Sub-contrary* of *Not all scientists are agnostics*:

(5) *Contradictory* of *No debutantes are ladies*:

(6) *Contrary* of *No women are astronauts*:

(7) *Sub-contrary* of *Some askari are beer-drinkers*:

(8) *Subaltern* of *All nurses are underpaid*:

(9) *Contrary* of *All guardian angels are saints*:

(10) *Contradictory* of *Some philosophers are not Thomists*:

B. In the spaces provided indicate the requested truth-value: TRUE, FALSE, UNKNOWN:

(1) If the *E* proposition is *TRUE*, then the *O* is . . . .

(2) If the *O* proposition is *FALSE*, then the *E* is . . . .

(3) If the *A* proposition is *FALSE*, then the *O* is . . . .

(4) If the *I* proposition is *FALSE*, then the *A* is . . . .

(5) If the *A* proposition is *FALSE*, and *E* is *FALSE*, then *I* is . . . . and *O* is . . . .

(6) If the *I* proposition is *TRUE*, then the *A* is . . . .

(7) If the *A* proposition is *TRUE*, then the *E* is . . . . , the *O* is . . . . , and the *I* is . . . .

(8) If the *O* proposition is *TRUE*, then the *E* is . . . . , the *I* is . . . . , and the *A* is . . . .

(9) If the *O* and *E* propositions are *FALSE*, then the *I* is . . . .

(10) If the *A* proposition is *TRUE* and the *E* is *FALSE*, then the *O* is . . . . and the *I* is . . . .

II. *Obversion and Conversion*

In the spaces provided, write the valid obverse form of the obvertend that is given:

(1) All non-Europeans are not non-Catholics:

(2) No Africans are noncolored:

(3) Every American is not impotent:

(4) Some astronauts are non-Russian:

(5) All political leaders are dishonest:

(6) Every war-monger is nonaltruistic:

(7) Not every collegian is athletic:

(8) Some physicists are mechanics:

(9) No mountain-climbers are nonvirile:

(10) Some teachers are not scholars:

(11) All poets are underpaid:

(12) No professional ballplayers in the U.S. are over-paid:

(13) All cross-country runners are not husky:

(14) Some rodents are rats:

(15) Every Christian is baptized:

III. *Contraposition*

In the spaces provided, give the necessary steps in contraposing the following propositions:

(1) All non-Europeans are not non-Catholics:

(2) Every American is not impotent:

(3) All political leaders are dishonest:

(4) Not every collegian is athletic:

(5) No mountain-climbers are nonvirile:

(6) All poets are underpaid:

(7) All cross-country runners are not husky:

(8) Every Christian is baptized:

IV. *General Review*

In the spaces provided, indicate the *truth-value* of these *properties* of the categorical propositions:

(1) If it is *TRUE* that *No soldiers are cowards*, then

    (a) Some soldiers are cowards, is . . . .

    (b) All soldiers are not cowards, is . . . .

    (c) All soldiers are noncowards, is . . . .

(2) If it is *FALSE* that *Not all businessmen are handsome*, then

    (a) All businessmen are not handsome, is . . . .

    (b) Some nonhandsome beings are not nonbusinessmen, is . . . .

    (c) No businessmen are handsome, is . . . .

    (d) No handsome beings are businessmen, is . . . .

(3) If it is *TRUE* that *No journalists are optimists*, then

    (a) No optimists are journalists, is . . . .

    (b) All journalists are nonoptimists, is . . . .

    (c) All optimists are nonjournalists, is . . . .

(d) All journalists are not optimists, is . . . .

(e) Not all journalists are optimists, is . . . .

(4) If it is *TRUE* that *All pacifists are nonpatriotic*,
then

(a) Some pacifists are nonpatriotic, is . . . .

(b) Not all pacifists are nonpatriotic, is . . . .

(c) No nonpatriotic people are
pacifists, is . . . .

(d) All patriotic people are nonpacifists, is . . . .

(5) If it is *FALSE* that *Some noncitizens are not Europeans*, then

(a) No Europeans are noncitizens, is . . . .

(b) No noncitizens are Europeans, is . . . .

(c) Some noncitizens are non-
Europeans, is . . . .

(d) Not all non-Europeans are
citizens, is . . . .

(6) If it is *FALSE* that *Some modern rulers are despots*, then

(a) Some despots are modern
rulers, is . . . .

     (b) No modern rulers are des-
          pots, is . . . .

     (c) All modern rulers are des-
          pots, is . . . .

     (d) No despots are modern
          rulers, is . . . .

(7) If it is *FALSE* that *All farmers are not rich*, then

     (a) All farmers are rich, is
        . . . .

     (b) Not all farmers are rich, is
        . . . .

     (c) No rich beings are farmers, is
        . . . .

     (d) No farmers are rich, is
        . . . .

     (e) Some nonrich beings are not
          nonfarmers, is . . . .

(8) If it is *TRUE* that *All athletes are muscular*, then

     (a) All nonmuscular beings are
          nonathletes, is . . . .

     (b) Some athletes are muscular,
          is . . . .

     (c) Not all athletes are muscular,
          is . . . .

     (d) Some nonmuscular beings
          are not nonathletes, is
        . . . .

     (e) No athletes are nonmuscular,
          is . . . .

(9) If it is *FALSE* that *Some bankers are capitalists*, then

 (a) No bankers are capitalists, is . . . .

 (b) Some capitalists are bankers, is . . . .

 (c) Some bankers are not non-capitalists, is . . . .

 (d) All bankers are capitalists, is . . . .

 (e) No bankers are noncapitalists, is . . . .

(10) If it is *TRUE* that *No courtesan is virtuous*, then

 (a) Every courtesan is virtuous, is . . . .

 (b) Some courtesans are virtuous, is . . . .

 (c) No virtuous being is a courtesan, is . . . .

 (d) Every courtesan is nonvirtuous, is . . . .

 (e) Every nonvirtuous being is a noncourtesan, is . . . .

7

Argumentation

The word "argumentative" has few if any pleasant connotations today. It is used most often of contentious and dogmatic persons. How the word came to take on such unflattering meaning we cannot explore in detail here. Nevertheless, when beginning a study of *argumentation,* we do well to remember how normal man's tendency to argue is; argumentation is both normal and natural for one who can desire to live a life that is both reasonable and sociable.

Most animals must settle their disputes and differences by fighting, but men have natural equipment with which to settle theirs by argumentation. The history of man is a witness to the truth that, despite their occasional warfare, men are naturally given to debate and discussion of the issues that seem to divide them. "Argumentative" has become pejorative in meaning because so many *arguers* have generated *heat* (of passion) when they should have generated *light* (of truth); genuine argumentation is impossible when the emotions dominate the mind.

Perhaps "guilt by association" is inevitable for *argumentation*; after all there must be some tension in this activity as in all man's other vital operations (e.g., between the metabolic and katabolic phases of the nutritive process). Argumentation, then, is a clear sign of vital mental operations. Traditionally, *argumentation* has had a primary meaning that is much more closely linked with science than with rhetoric, with enlightening than with convincing. Its chief objective under normal conditions is to enable men to understand better some facet of being and truth and goodness, even to have certitude about them. Basically, then, argumentation is not a logical weapon to be employed by hotheads or sophists to beat down opponents; rather, it is the natural sign of men's indigenous power to grow in reasoning by gaining multidimensional insights into reality.

Since there is so much misunderstanding about the nature and purposes of argumentation, this chapter will attempt to dissipate some of it in three ways: (1) by a brief analysis of the functional factors in the act of reasoning which is so basic to argumentation of any sort; (2) by a quick examination of the inductive form of reasoning; and (3) by a study in-depth of the most perfect form of deductive reasoning, the categorical syllogistic, as conceived theoretically by Aristotle some 2000 years ago. Then in the next chapter the principles and norms of *validity* for the categorical syllogism will be considered.

I

Because they are so natural to human beings, *acts of reasoning* are truly satisfying and enjoyable experiences. Though a bit taxing at times, ratiocination or conceptual thinking can on occasion even be fun. Like most human functions, the act of reasoning is also complex. It begins with simple conceptualizations of things derived from sensory perceptions; the human mind is then consciously moved to analyze and compare these ideas or concepts. As we saw in a previous chapter, the logical entity known as the *proposition* is the sign of this phase of the operation; these actions are, as it were, the seeds from which the act of reasoning itself is an outgrowth. Then the *discursive* features of the intellect become more apparent in its step-by-step procedure in arriving at conclusions, which are simply the result of comparing judgments or propositions. Reasoning, in short, is a genuine movement of the intellect involving a *mediate inference*, one that is a bit complicated since it is based on a comparison of two or more mutually-relevant judgments or propositions.[1]

Perhaps an illustration will help to make this analysis of the factors involved in a mediate inference clearer: (if) all men are persons, (and if) all neighbors are men, (then) all neighbors are persons. In this argument a relatively new truth is inferred in the conclusion *All neighbors are persons*: some new notion relative to the first two statements has been brought over to the third statement. Such a movement in logic is said to be a *mediate inference* or *mediate illation*. Because no creature can "create" (i.e., make something out of absolute nothingness), the conclusion *All neighbors are persons* must have been contained to some extent in the statements (called the *antecedent* in logic) from which it was inferred. Hence, it is evident that something less apparent in the antecedent is made more apparent in the conclusion (called the *consequent* in logic) through a complex, unobservable act of inference (called the *consequence* in logic).

It might be profitable for us to reflect here on the fact that logicians unanimously agree that every act of reasoning, regardless of the matter or meaning signified by the terms employed in the propositions involved in the discursive movement, consists necessarily of an inferential or an illative factor. Yet not every inferential or illative act is logically good or correct. Like buildings constructed in violation of approved principles of architecture and of engineering, many arguments suffer from having a logically bad or incorrect *consequence*.

Logicians are also in agreement that *in a good consequence an antecedent that is true and a consequent* (*conclusion*) *that is false cannot be logically valid, and that if the antecedent is true, so too is the consequent* (*conclusion*). In these related axioms are reflected the primary principles of sound reasoning. Unless these logical conditions are satisfied in every act of reasoning, the inferential or illative operation (the act of consequence) will be logically defective because its important role of uniting the antecedent and the consequent would not have been fulfilled. In other words, the inference or illation would be more apparent than real.[2] To prevent such mistakes in ratiocination is the help provided by Logic, inasmuch as it is a cooperative art.

II

Before we examine the *inductive* form of reasoning as one of the two types or classes of argumentation, it will be feasible for us to see some of the features common to both types or classes of argumentation. Logicians generally define "argumentation" as a kind of perfect composite expression in which one thing having been given, something else follows. This definition has three major parts, each of which can be briefly described as follows: (a) Since an argument is constructed from propositions or truth-value statements which in themselves generate a complete meaning, and since the acts of comparing and inferring are essential factors in every act of reasoning, an argument is a logical artifact that is rightly said to be *a kind of perfect composite expression*; (b) The expression *one thing having been given* in the definition has direct reference to the argument's "antecedent," which consists of two or more interrelated propositional statements containing some *common term* being compared with other terms, usually two in number; (c) The expression *something else follows* is the part of the definition that aptly describes the argument's "consequent" or "conclusion" resulting from the inference or illation, a necessary element in any type of argument. The objective of *argumentation*, then, is to draw out a new truth from what is already contained explicitly or implicitly in related premises through some logically correct consequence.

Induction or inductive reasoning is a logically valid procedure of argumentation for arriving at new truths. As a conventional form of argumentation, it provides a very popular and useful methodology for those sciences dealing mostly with material entities (e.g., chemistry, psychology, mathematical physics). Most inductive arguments tend to be *a posteriori* in character, insofar as their normal plan of operation is to fashion a quasi-universal law or formula only after a rather exhaustive study of singular entities' actions and reactions. Such a procedure can be truly scientific inasmuch as the actions of a thing usually indicate its nature (*agere sequitur esse*). The potential of induction as a logical methodology is still being explored by scientists. In a subsequent chapter its perfections and limitations will be studied and evaluated.[3]

III

(a)

Deduction also is a logically valid procedure for coming to the knowledge of new truths. As a form of argumentation, it has been employed effectively and frequently by such disparate sciences as mathematics and theology. Deductive argumentation is more or less *a prioristic* in its procedure, moving from the more universal to the less universal. As a popular and valid methodology it can be seen in its crystallized form in the Aristotelian syllogistic (e.g.: "If A is predicated of all B, and B of all C, A must be predicated of all C; similarly: if A of no B, and B of all C, it is necessary that no C will be A").[4] The remaining sections of this chapter will be directly concerned with the basic notions of the Stagirite's theory of the categorical or assertoric syllogism. In a subsequent chapter the noncategorical or compound syllogism will be given both a traditional and a modern presentation.

(b)

In the early chapters of his treatise *Prior Analytics I*, Aristotle systematically exposed his teaching on the categorical syllogism. The Peripatetic Philosopher, as Aristotle (384–322 B.C.) is commonly known, is recognized by historians of logic as the most important pioneer theorist of syllogistic reasoning. But his theory has over the centuries received a strange mixture of criticism.

Recently I. M. Bochenski, O.P., an internationally famous

logician, asserted that in Aristotle's syllogistic are found "three of the greatest discoveries of our science."[5] Another widely-known scholar in the field of logic, W. D. Ross, claims that the Peripatetic was truly "the originator of formal logic" and that his theory of the syllogism is the "greatest of his achievements as a logician."[6] Logician Jan Lukasiewicz credits Aristotle with having had a remarkable influence on the arithmetical studies of his day by introducing the use of *term-variables* (e.g., "B" and "C" in the categorical proposition "No B is C") into his syllogistic.[7] Praise for this novel creation does not, however, belong exclusively to the Stagirite. Most scholars now believe that he was influenced in some phases of his theory of the syllogism by other savants of his time, principally by Plato, who was his tutor for almost twenty years.[8]

For more than 2000 years, this logical invention as a construct for sound reasoning, namely the syllogism, has been subjected also to severe attacks and to scholarly questioning. Its probative value has been seriously and frequently challenged. Still, highly reputable logicians have constantly come to the defense of Aristotle's syllogistic as a valid method of inference against the charge that it is *circular*, a kind of petitio principii. Not a little of the criticism over the years has had good results insofar as many of the limitations, textual obscurities, and structural defects of Aristotle's theory have been painstakingly revealed by the work of scholars.[9]

These historical facts should be neither disturbing nor surprising to beginners in logic. One must not forget that the Stagirite was an innovator, a pioneering theorist who was in effect blazing a trail in a relatively unexplored and poorly-mapped area of scientific methodology. Perhaps some of his severest critics have been forgetful of this fact. In any field of learning, whether it be logic, mathematics, aerodynamics, or electrical engineering, there is little to be gained by denigrating the accomplishments of early theorists. No well-informed follower of Aristotelian logic will deny that his syllogistic has its limitations; at the same time an appreciation of its virtues enables one to see Aristotle's contributions to logic in true proportions.

(c)

Besides the "demythologizing" of the syllogistic as a logical theory, Aristotle's writings on this subject have also been variously *interpreted* by scholars. This is not to be unexpected. The writings of most early theorists, after undergoing a literary and a scientific analysis, inevitably receive a variety of interpretations from commentators—interpretations often hardly imagined by the original authors. The *Prior Analytics* has occasioned a great number of interpretations because of its many ambiguous statements and incomplete texts. Sometimes, Aristotle failed to distinguish clearly in his writings between the formalities of the syllogistic and its practical application. Though there are many shades of differences between scholarly interpretations of his theory of the syllogism, for the sake of simplicity we will consider them under two general heads: (i) *the traditional interpretation* and (ii) *the nontraditional interpretation*.

The *traditional interpretation* of the categorical syllogism tends to stress its *inferential* factor. The advocates of this interpretation consider the rules of inference of supreme importance and give minimal attention to the feature of axiomatization or the use of term-variables in the theory. For them the categorical syllogism is a rather static thing in which two propositions, called the *antecedent*, are juxtaposed and, through a logically correct act of inference (the consequence), yield another categorical proposition called the *conclusion* or *consequent*. In this interpretation the inferential act (*the consequence*) is symbolized in one of three conventional ways: by a line called a *stroke* (——————); by the word *therefore*; or by three dots arranged triangularly (∴):

> All zebras are animals.
>
> @ Some pets are zebras.
>
> ——————
>
> Some pets are animals.

All C is B.

@ All C is A.

Therefore (or ∴) Some A is B

The *nontraditional interpretation* of the categorical syllogism tends to stress its *implicational* or *conditional* factor, i.e., *if then*. In this interpretation, logical laws and axiomatization are emphasized. Generally familiar with the rigorous procedures of symbolic logic, advocates of the nontraditional interpretation are prone to analyze and criticize Aristotle's theory of the syllogism chiefly from that frame of reference. Apparent in their interpretations are often inaccurate attributions to Aristotle of things that cannot be found literally in his writings, either to his credit or discredit. They desire to see the categorical syllogism constructed along the *implicational* lines of modern logic so that the intimate relationships between antecedent and consequent will be apparent, as in the following examples:

If all B is A

antecedent

and all C is B

then all C is A.   *consequent*

If some A belongs to all B,

antecedent

and some B belongs to all C,

therefore some A belongs to all C.   *consequent*

If all broad-leaved plants are deciduous,

antecedent

and all vines are broad-leaved plants,

then all vines are deciduous.[10]   *consequent*

Having examined briefly the two major schools of interpretation of the syllogistic and seen the ways in which it has undergone modification in practice, we shall find it convenient and more meaningful to formulate syllogisms in the rest of this presentation in a manner that combines the best features of these interpretations. In doing so we will have the support of many Aristotelian scholars, especially A. N. Prior, who asserts that "the implicative forms which Aristotle uses are a perfectly natural way of talking *about* syllogisms (asserting their validity), but a statement *about* a syllogism is not itself a syllogism; and on the few occasions when Aristotle gives actual examples which he calls syllogisms, they are not implications but inferences.[11] Hence we shall formulate categorical syllogisms in the following way:

> (If) all B is A,
>
> (and if) all C is B,
>
> (*then-therefore*) all C is A.

(d)

Like any artifact, the categorical syllogism has a distinctive form or structure consisting of the various dispositions capable of being given to its *propositions* and *terms*. Regardless of *what* these propositions enunciate and these terms signify, propositions and terms make up, as it were, the *form* or *framework* of the standardized categorical syllogism. Each of these factors is now to be examined.

(i) *Propositions* are interrelated categorical statements or propositional-forms (e.g., Not all apples are red; No x is y), usually three in number per syllogism. In theorizing, Aristotle was wont to employ term-variables (such as "A" for ants and "E" for edible) in the propositional statements of the categorical syllogism. In applying the syllogistic to the practical order, he generally employed the concrete terms of universal character with which men are familiar (e.g., vines, zebras, plants, animals).

The *first two* propositions appearing in the categorical syllogism are commonly referred to as *premises,* for they are truth-valued statements affirming or denying some attribute of something else. Taken as a logical unit, these two premises are customarily known by logicians as the *antecedent* of the syllogism, i.e., "the certain things being given" of the definition of the syllogism. The third or last categorical proposition that appears in the syllogism is called the *consequent* or *conclusion* because it has been drawn from the antecedent by the act of inference which is commonly known as the *consequence,* i.e., for "other things *necessarily* follow."

The *antecedent* consists of the *major premise* and the *minor premise,* both of which are categorical or simple propositions: (i) The *major* premise will generally be first in position and will ordinarily contain the predicate-term of the conclusion and the middle-term of the syllogism itself. (ii) The *minor* premise will generally be second in position and will ordinarily contain the subject-term of the conclusion and the middle-term of the syllogism itself. The *consequent* or the *conclusion* will always contain only the *extremes* of the syllogism, *never the middle-term.*

Each proposition in the categorical syllogism will be one of these types of categorical propositions: *A, E, I, O.* Singular and indefinite propositions, as indicated in a previous chapter, can ordinarily be reduced to one of these types. In passing, attention may be called here to the rather peculiar idiom employed by Aristotle (or the translations into English) in stating these four classes of categorical propositions in his theory: e.g., M *belongs to* all N and to some O; A *is predicated of* no B.

The logical form of every categorical syllogism depends a great deal on what is called its *mood.* The mood of every categorical syllogism is determined solely by the quality and quantity of each of the categorical propositions that constitute it. Employing the traditional symbols *A, E, I,* and *O,* we can express the logical mood of any categorical syllogism by indicating the sequence in which the propositions appear: *A-A-A, E-A-E, E-O-I,* etc. There are *sixteen* moods possible in each of the four so-called "logical figures" (or, schema), which we shall examine later in this chapter. To appreciate just what logical figures are and how they are constructed presupposes a knowledge of the part played by the terms of the categorical syllogism.

(ii) *Terms* are likewise the formal logical elements into which the categorical propositions of the categorical syllogism can be resolved. As mentioned earlier, the Stagirite was wont to use term-variables in his theorizing because of their value as substitutes for any number of concrete terms, such as *dogs* and *cats*. In the standardized categorical syllogism there are generally *only three terms* that appear, regardless of their many possible positions. These terms are traditionally known as the *major extreme*, the *minor extreme*, and the *middle-term*. Logicians who have studied the problem are in almost unanimous agreement that it is quite difficult to find a totally unambiguous and universally acceptable definition of any of these syllogistic terms in the *Prior Analytics*.[12] Perhaps this might be the result of Aristotle's preoccupation with the ideal way such terms are used in the first, or most perfect, logical "figure." Nevertheless, the following descriptions are offered only as functional definitions of each of these terms in the light of the textual ambiguities.

The *major extreme* is usually the term other than the middle-term in the major or first premise. In the "perfect" logical figure (i.e., the *first*), it is the predicate-term in relation to the middle-term, and also the predicate-term in the conclusion. It is likewise the syllogistic term that enjoys the greatest universality of extension, such as the term *honest* in this categorical syllogism:

(If) every man is *honest*,

(and if) every citizen is a man,

(*then-therefore*) every citizen is *honest*.

The *minor extreme* is usually the term other than the middle-term in the minor or second premise. In the "perfect" logical figure (i.e., the *first*), it is the subject-term in relation to the middle-term, and also the subject-term in the conclusion. It is likewise the syllogistic term that enjoys the least universality of extension, such as the term-variable *a* in the following categorical syllogism:

> (If) no c is b,
>
> (and if) all *a* is c,
>
> (*then-therefore*) no *a* is b.

The *middle-term* is often compared to the fulcrum of a see-saw, for it provides a kind of "balance" and unity for the categorical syllogism. It can be used without restriction in the place usually occupied by the subject-term and the predicate-term in each premise or both premises of the syllogism; but it is *never* found in the conclusion of a validly constructed categorical syllogism. One logician describes it this way: "the two equiform terms that occur only in the premises are called middle terms."[13] Only in the first logical figure does this term normally enjoy the median of universality of extension as the term *chickens* does in this categorical syllogism:

> (If) all *chickens* are egg-layers,
>
> (and if) all Rhode Island reds are *chickens*,
>
> (*then-therefore*) all Rhode Island reds are egg-layers.

In determining the "logical figure" of any categorical syllogism, we need to consider only the *position* of its middle-term. There are *four* distinct positions to which it can be assigned in the syllogistic. Most scholars agree that Aristotle was not unaware of the possibility of the fourth figure, for he employed it more than once in the *Analytics*; but he explicitly taught his syllogistic only in three logical figures (schemata). It has been suggested that he neglected to treat the fourth logical figure formally, mostly because of the way imperfections, with respect to the terms, escalated in logical figures two and three. According to some of the scholars, too, there is little or no evidence to support the view that Galen, a second-century physician, was the originator of this controversial fourth logical figure of the normal three-term categorical syllogism.[14]

There are, then, these *four distinct positions* that the middle-term is capable of taking in the categorical syllogistic:

(1) In the *first* logical figure, the middle-term is the subject-term of the major premise and the predicate-term of the minor premise:

> (If) all *A* are B,
>
> (and if) some C are *A*,
>
> (*then-therefore*) not all C are B.

(2) In the *second* logical figure, the middle-term is the predicate-term of both premises:

> (If) all M are *X*,
>
> (and if) no N are *X*,
>
> (*then-therefore*) no N are M.

(3) In the *third* logical figure, the middle-term is the subject-term of both premises:

> (If) not every *Z* is Y,
>
> (and if) every *Z* is X,
>
> (*then-therefore*) not every X is Y.

(4) In the *fourth* logical figure, the middle-term is the predicate-term of the major premise and the subject-term of the minor premise:

> (If) no A is *B*,
>
> (and if) some *B* are C,
>
> (*then-therefore*) not every C is A.

Pertinent Quotations about argumentation:

(a)

Argumentation, moreover, is called a total composite expression made up of premises and conclusion. In that the power of the argument is manifested because one can infer the universal or the particular, and either affirmative or negative, as was stated earlier.

> —Peter of Spain (Pope John XXI), *Summulae Logicales*, bk. VII, tract V (author's translation).

(b)

The human intellect must of necessity understand by composition and division. For since the intellect passes from potentiality to act, it has a likeness to things which are generated, which do not attain to perfection all at once but acquire it by degrees: so likewise the human intellect does not acquire perfect knowledge by the first act of apprehension; but it first apprehends something about its object, such as its quiddity, and this is its first and proper object; and then it understands the properties, accidents, and the various relations of the essence. Thus it necessarily compares one thing with another by composition and division; and from one composition and division it proceeds to another, which is the *process of reasoning*.

> —St. Thomas Aquinas, *Summa Theologica*, part I, quest. 85, art. 5, tr. Fathers of the English Dominican Province (New York: Benziger Bros., 1947).

(c)

That *consequence* is called *good,* in which the antecedent infers the consequent. Moreover, that is a *bad consequence* in which the consequent (conclusion) is not inferred from the antecedent, although it may be signified that it was inferred. Then, the consequent is really not inferred from some antecedent when it can be given that the antecedent is *true* and the consequent *false*. However, when a true consequent is drawn out by a genuine illation, either from a true or false antecedent, such a consequence is good. . . .

Since the essential and intrinsic form of the *consequence* is the illative connection of the antecedent with the consequent (conclusion), and since this illative force is lacking in the bad consequence, it follows that in such instances the genuine form so essential to the ontic nature of a logical consequence is missing. Therefore, a *good consequence* differs from a bad consequence in a somewhat similar way that a living man differs from a lifeless one.

> —John of St. Thomas, *Cursus phil. Thomisticus*, "Logica," part I, illustr. art. 1 (author's translation).

(d)

A *syllogism* is discourse in which, certain things being stated, something other than what is stated follows of necessity from their being so. I mean by the last phrase that they produce the consequence, and by this, that no further term is required from without in order to make the consequence necessary.

I call that a *perfect syllogism* which needs nothing other than what has been stated to make plain what necessarily follows; a syllogism is *imperfect,* if it needs either one or more propositions, which are indeed the necessary consequences of the terms set down, but have not been expressly stated as premises.

That one *term* should be included in another as in a whole is the same as for the other to be predicated of all of the first. And we say that one term is predicated of all of another, whenever no instance of the subject can be found of which the other term cannot be asserted: *to be predicated of none* must be understood in the same way.

> —*The Basic Works of Aristotle*, tr. R. McKeon (New York: Random House, 1941), "Prior Analytics I," ch. 1; by permission of the Clarendon Press, Oxford.

(e)

Truly indeed it seems that the *syllogism* in its very essential notion *signifies a discourse* comprised of the antecedent, the consequent, and their consequence. Thus, it contains both an illative potentiality, which is present in the premises, and something actually inferred, which is in the conclusion. Added to these is the illative act itself, which passively is present in the conclusion as drawn and actively in the premises as inferable. And so the syllogism is a kind of organic instrument, composed of a *moving part* and a *moved part,* as in living things one part moves another part. Thus it is that the premises themselves are the motivating factor and the reason the conclusion gets to be known.

> —John of St. Thomas, *Cursus phil. Thomisticus,* "Logica," part I, illustr. quest. 8, art. 3 (author's translation).

(f)

When pure mathematics is organized as a *deductive* system—i.e., as the set of all those propositions that can be deduced from an assigned set of premises—it becomes obvious that, if we are to believe in the truth of pure mathematics, it cannot be solely because we believe in the truth of the set of premises. Some of the premises are much less obvious than some of their consequences, and are believed chiefly because of their consequences. This will be found to be always the case when a science is arranged as a deductive system. It is not the logically simplest propositions of the system that are the most obvious, or that provide the chief part of our reasons for believing in the system. With the empirical sciences this is evident. Electro-dynamics, for example, can be concentrated into Maxwell's equations, but these equations are believed because of the observed truth of certain of their logical consequences. Exactly the same thing happens in the pure realm of logic; the logically first principles of logic—at least some of them—are to be believed, not on their own account, but on account of their *consequences.*

> —Bertrand Russell, *Logic and Knowledge: Essays 1901–1950,* ed. Robert Charles Marsh (New York: The Macmillan Co., 1956), p. 325.

Exercise:

In the spaces provided, indicate the logical *figure* and *mood* of each of these categorical syllogisms:

(1) *Figure*: .... (If) all sailors are handsome,

    Mood: .... (and if) no sailors are misanthropes, (*then-therefore*) no handsome beings are misanthropes.

(2) *Figure*: .... (If) all automobiles are expensive,

    Mood: .... (and if) some expensive things are rare, (*then-therefore*) some things are automobiles.

(3) *Figure*: .... (If) all R are not S,

    Mood: .... (and if) some Q are S, (*then-therefore*) some Q are not R.

(4) *Figure*: .... (If) all demonstrations are valid,

    Mood: .... (and if) not all syllogisms are valid, (*then-therefore*) some syllogisms are not demonstrations.

(5) *Figure*: .... (If) all nurses are underpaid,

    Mood: .... (and if) no underpaid beings are scientists, (*then-therefore*) no scientists are nurses.

(6) *Figure*: . . . . (If) no beatniks are virile,

    Mood: . . . . (and if) some golfers are not virile, (*then-therefore*) not all golfers are beatniks.

(7) *Figure*: . . . . (If) every soldier is courageous,

    Mood: . . . . (and if) no soldier is a hippie, (*then-therefore*) no hippie is courageous.

(8) *Figure*: . . . . (If) all hyenas are odoriferous,

    Mood: . . . . (and if) some untamed animals are hyenas, (*then-therefore*) some untamed animals are odoriferous.

(9) *Figure*: . . . . (If) all nuns are religious,

    Mood: . . . . (and if) some religious are not women, (*then-therefore*) some women are not nuns.

(10) *Figure*: . . . . (If) all x are not y,

    Mood: . . . . (and if) all x are z, (*then-therefore*) not all z are y.

8
Validity of Categorical Syllogisms

In countries where the medium of exchange is coin or paper note, money that has not been issued by the authorized source is considered counterfeit. A country that lacked safeguards for checking and protecting the integrity of its currency would be in constant danger of economic collapse. Anyone who has ever had the sad experience of receiving counterfeit money while traveling in a foreign country knows well how deceptive is its appearance and how impotent its purchasing power.

There is a parallel between a nation's monetary system and discourse among men. If no norms existed by which the logical worth of arguments could be objectively evaluated, one could not tell valid arguments from invalid ones—a most frustrating state of affairs, if that were the case, because men have a natural inclination both to know the truth and to communicate it. That norms do exist is made evident to us in contemporary society by such events as labor disputes, divorce court proceedings, decisions of the Supreme Court, prolix discussions of international dimensions carried on at U.N. meetings, etc. In short, men do not act as if all arguments were equally *valid* or acceptable in rational discourse.

Logicians, of course, are professionally sensitive to the inequity of arguments; their primary concern with any argument or alleged proof is its formal or structural aspects, not its content-matter. They decide the logical value of an argument according to its "structural lines." Since *validity* is the paramount concern of the logician, this chapter will explore three topics related to the validity of categorical syllogisms: (1) the means for testing the logical value (i.e., validity) of all categorical arguments whether they are proposed conventionally or not; (2) the procedures for bolstering valid arguments in figures other than the first by the *reductive* process;[1] and (3) the two major types of informal syllogistic argumentation, the *enthymeme* and the *sorites*.

I

(a)

Aristotle made it very evident in his *Analytics* that not all categorical syllogisms are of equal logical value. His assessments, however, were the result neither of personal whim nor of guess-work, but were formulated along scientific lines. For assaying arguments cast in the form of the categorical syllogism, he recognized the need for rigorous logical standards. His concern for a set of objective and invariable norms is clearly reflected in his theory of syllogistic reasoning.

In the axiomatization of the categorical syllogistic, the Stagirite ultimately depended on nothing less than a few indisputable principles as a foundation upon which to erect a superstructure of logical laws, axioms, and rules. Still, he did not intend to make the categorical syllogistic an *end* in itself. The principal purpose to be served by the categorical syllogism was simply *scientific knowledge*, which demonstration guaranteed: ". . . . syllogism should be discussed before demonstration, because syllogism is the more general: the demonstration is a sort of syllogism, but not every syllogism is a demonstration."[2]

But this ambitious objective would hardly have been realizable unless his theory of the categorical syllogism was well grounded in *being*, i.e., in those universal, most certain, and indemonstrable truths implicitly agreed upon by all men who believe in the possibility of genuine proofs.[3] Aristotle explicitly states two primary principles pertinent both to the real and the logical orders of being: (1) that everything must be either affirmed or denied; (2) that the same thing cannot at one and the same time be and not be, or admit any other similar pair of opposites.[4] He assigns less dignity to such common truths as the *law of the excluded middle* and the axiom "take equals from equals and equals remain."[5]

However, the *proximate basis* of Aristotle's axiomatization of his notions on the syllogism is a set or group of logical laws and axioms from which the general logical norms for evaluating all categorical syllogisms are derived. These logical laws are traditionally known as the *law of opposition* and the *law of conversion*. Throughout the *Analytics*, the Peripatetic refers to them as *principles of validation*. Both these laws we have already explained and applied in an earlier chapter (ch. 6). To minimize their importance in the categorical syllogistic is certainly to distort Aristotle's theory of the syllogism.

Most Aristotelian logicians are agreed that some special *dicta* or *axioms*, such as the *dictum de omni* and the *dictum de nullo*, also play a relatively important role in the categorical syllogistic.[6] In the formal presentation of his theory in the first chapter of *Prior Analytics I*, Aristotle clearly admits the relevance of these axioms to his logical system: "that one term should be included in another as in a whole is the same as for the other to be predicated of all of the first. And we say that one term is predicated of all of another, whenever no instance of the subject can be found of which the other term cannot be asserted: *to be predicated of none* must be understood in the same way." For example, the axiom *dictum de omni* ("to be predicated of all") means that whatever is affirmed universally of a class or a set (e.g., *man*) can be affirmed of each and every individual in that class or set; whereas the axiom *dictum de nullo* ("to be predicated of none") means whatever is denied universally of a class or a set (e.g., *horse*) should be denied of each and every individual in that class or set.

(b)

Having seen the rational foundations of Aristotle's theory of the categorical syllogism, we must now examine the norms for its *validity* in detail. There are only *five* logical rules for determining the logical value of a categorical syllogistic form (i.e., its validity or invalidity). To these derived logical rules or standards, which are not completely independent of each other, all valid categorical syllogistic arguments must conform. In short, a logically defective (i.e., invalid) categorical syllogism will result from the infraction of one or more of the five rules. Such an infraction necessarily renders a syllogistic form invalid, regardless of its content-matter. These five logical rules are clearly stated in the *Analytics* as a procedure for determining the *validity* of every logical figure.[7]

Rule 1—It must be composed of only three terms. Observance of this first rule is absolutely necessary for validity, regardless of the logical figure into which the two premises housing the three terms are cast. This necessity is a logical result of the relationship of dependence of the conclusion upon the antecedent. Since the conclusion of the categorical syllogism explicitly signifies that a *relationship* (positive or negative) obtains between two of the three terms (viz., the major extreme and the minor extreme), their mutual reference to the same *middle-term* must have been already established in its premises. Otherwise the very purpose of the syllogism would be unfulfilled or even frustrated. Aristotle explicitly states that this rule concerning the number of term-variables is basic to the very structure of the categorical syllogism.[8]

On the other hand, if any categorical syllogism has less than or more than *three* term-variables, there could be no suitable comparison or judicial inference by which a new truth would be drawn out. Any of the possible fallacies that result from the violation of this syllogistic rule of validity will be avoided only if the unity of signification and supposition of each of the three term-variables is not altered. However, in most instances of this infraction, it is the *middle-term* that is most likely, if most subtly, to undergo alteration in signification. It happens not infrequently that the middle-term is given, designedly or not, a dual suppositional value in the premises, i.e., by using a verbal-signifier in *proper* supposition in one premise and in *improper* supposition in the other premise. Any form of equivocation must also be kept clear of if this first rule is to be observed. Some examples of how this rule can be violated follow:

(If) all *men* are rational animals,

(and if) no women are *men*,

(*then-therefore*) no women are rational animals.

Comment: The middle-term, *men*, is being used in the major premise so as to apply in an *unrestricted sense* to all individuals sharing formally in humanity; but in the minor premise the same term is being used only in a *genderic sense*. Therefore, there are more than three terms.

(If) every *lion* is irrational,

(and if) Christ is a *lion* (of Juda),

(*then-therefore*) Christ is irrational.

Comment: The middle-term, *lion,* enjoys *proper supposition* in the major premise, but only *improper supposition* (metaphor) in the minor premise. Thus the middle-term is taken in two different senses, causing the syllogism to have more than three terms.

(If) all *coaches* (on a certain railroad line) are unclean,

(and if) some persons at Hardknock College are *coaches*,

(*then-therefore*) some persons at Hardknock College are unclean.

Comment: This syllogism provides a clear case of equivocation in the middle-term, *coaches*, for in the minor premise the designation is to those engaged in coaching dramatics, sports, debating, etc.

Rule 2—The middle-term must be distributed at least once. This logical rule is probably the most important of the five. Aristotle writes plainly about its functional importance in valid argumentation: ". . . we know that a syllogism cannot be drawn without a middle-term, and that term which is stated more than once is the middle."[9] This rule should not be difficult for us to apply, for we have already analyzed each element contained in it; in applying it, however, we should keep three things in mind: (1) the middle-term is, as it were, the hinge on which the categorical syllogism swings or the fulcrum on which it is balanced; (2) any term-variable in a categorical proposition is said to be *distributed* only when its extension is complete or universal; and (3) in Aristotle's system of logic, the *subject-term* of any standardized *A* and *E* categorical proposition and the *predicate-term* of any standardized *E* and *O* categorical proposition possess the fullness of *distribution*.

The second rule requires, then, that in each and every valid categorical syllogism *all* of the *middle-term* must be signified *at least once* in the antecedent or premises so that the consequent or conclusion can be justified in asserting the relationship (positive or negative) between the *extremes* of the syllogism. This logical canon guarantees the scientific feature of the categorical syllogistic as a genuine methodology, for there is no "science" of particulars. *Science*, in its strict sense, designates a knowledge of *universals*.[10] Only when the middle-term is used at least once in a total and universal sense in the antecedent or premises will this rule be observed, and scientific conclusions be produced.

On the other hand, whenever the middle-term is *undistributed* in both premises of a categorical syllogism, it takes on an indefiniteness and incompleteness that generates only ambiguity and does not objectively justify asserting a genuine connection between its extremes. Because it is possible for the extremes to be each connected with or have reference to a *different segment* of the middle-term, they need not be connected at all with each other. The following syllogisms violate the second rule of validity:

> (If) all zebras are *animals,*
>
> (and if) all men are *animals,*
>
> (*then-therefore*) all men are zebras.
>
> *Comment*: The middle-term, *animals,* has an incomplete or undistributive signification in both premises; thus this syllogisitc form is *invalid,* for the middle-term lacks the universality needed for validity.

> (If) not every X is Y,
>
> (and if) every Z is $X,$
>
> (*then-therefore*) not every Z is Y.
>
> *Comment*: The middle-term, $X,$ is not taken even once *distributively,* i.e., in an universal sense; thus this argument-form is invalid also.

> (If) all M are $N,$
>
> (and if) some N are O,
>
> (*then-therefore*) some O are M.
>
> *Comment*: The middle-term, $N,$ in this fourth figure categorical syllogism is *undistributed* in both premises; thus any syllogistic form that lacks universality of denotation in its middle-term is necessarily *invalid.*

Rule 3—Overdistribution of an extreme in the conclusion is always prohibited. This third rule is the one most frequently, and even flagrantly, trespassed in everyday social intercourse. Trespasses occur whenever people try to prove more than is warranted by their premises—a logical maneuver not unlike attempting to put too much air in a balloon, except that the balloon inevitably manifests the excess of air by bursting; such "inflated" syllogisms often go undetected by the logically unwary.

Those who ignore this logical norm endeavor, knowingly or unknowingly, to give a quantity of extensionality to either extreme in the conclusion greater than it possesses in the antecedent. In other words, because the premises potentially contain the conclusion in any valid categorical syllogism, it follows that any conclusion would be *over-extending* itself by declaring more about either extreme than is stated or implied in the antecedent. This rule is, therefore, nothing else than a logical reflection of the principle that, naturally speaking, no effect is greater than its cause. He who violates this logical canon by attempting to prove too much ends by proving nothing.

This rule requires that a term-variable, if employed *in a limited or particularized sense* in the antecedent of a categorical syllogism, should not be employed in an universalized or distributed sense in the consequent. Aristotle offers many examples of this kind of logical invalidity in the *Analytics*. His very first example is this: "but if the first term belongs to all the middle, but the middle to none of the last term, there will be no syllogism in respect of the extremes; for nothing necessary follows from the terms being so related; for it is possible that the first should belong either to all or to none of the last, so that neither a particular nor a universal conclusion is necessary. But if there is no necessary consequence, there cannot be a syllogism by means of these premises."[11] In the following examples, the first presents this argument just stated in syllogistic form, and the second is an invalid syllogism in the fourth figure:

> (If) every X is Y,
>
> (and if) no Z is X,
>
> (*then-therefore*) no Z is Y.
>
> *Comment*: The major extreme, Y, is undistributed in the major premise, but appears *distributed* in the conclusion, for the predicate-term of a negative categorical proposition

is always distributed; thus such a syllogistic form trespasses the third rule.

(If) all X is Y,

(and if) all Y is Z,

(*then-therefore*) all Z is X.

Comment: Though the Stagirite did not formally treat the fourth figure of the categorical syllogistic, this rule is not less applicable to it, since the minor extreme, Z, is *undistributed* in the minor premise, yet appears *distributed* in the consequent. Such a procedure is logically invalid in virtue of this third rule.

Rule 4—Every antecedent must be composed of one universal premise and one affirmative premise. Most manuals of traditional logic state this rule somewhat differently, usually in these words: *from two negative premises or from two particular premises nothing validly follows.* There is no substantive difference in the meaning of this rule; our preferred wording of this logical canon, however, is that explicitly enunciated by Aristotle many times in the *Analytics*, viz.: "Further in every syllogism one of the premises must be affirmative, and universality must be present: unless one of the premises is universal either a syllogism will not be possible, or it will not refer to the subject proposed, or the original position will be begged."[12]

It sometimes happens that a true consequent is derived from two negative premises; but a consequent so derived does not come about in any necessary or probative manner, for both extremes are denied of or separated from the *middle-term*. There is, then, no basis for any logical connection between the antecedent and the consequent, as the following syllogism illustrates:

(If) no *mineral* is an angel,

(and if) no elephant is a *mineral*,

(*then-therefore*) no elephant is an angel.

> *Comment*: Because both extremes are denied of the middle-term, *mineral*, no identity of the extremes is established at all in order to prove the consequent, which happens to be true but does not logically follow from these premises.

Aristotle also phrases this rule negatively, thus: "nor is a syllogism possible when both are stated in the negative, but one is universal, the other particular."[13] A basic reason Aristotle repeatedly offers for the necessity of there being a universal premise in every *valid* categorical syllogism is the indefinite nature of the particular proposition. This aspect of the fourth rule is not unrelated to the other logical rules concerned with *distribution*, for distribution problems would usually arise from any two particular premises. He very plainly says: "nor can there in any way be a syllogism if both the relations of subject and predicate are particular, either positively or negatively, or the one negative and the other affirmative, or one indefinite and the other definite, or both indefinite."[14] Perhaps two classical examples of syllogisms that *conform* to the fourth rule will demonstrate this rule's importance:

> (If) no X is Y,
>
> (and if) all Z is X,
>
> (*then-therefore*) no Z is Y.

> *Comment*: In this syllogistic both conditions required by Rule 4, *affirmation* and *universality*, are present. The quality of the universal premise is optional, but an affirmative premise in the antecedent is necessary. Sometimes, as in an *A* proposition, both requirements are adequately satisfied in one and the same premise.

> (If) no M is N,
>
> (and if) some N is O,
>
> (*then-therefore*) not all O is M.

> *Comment*: In this instance, too, both conditions are present, *affirmation* and *universality*. The quality of the

universal premise is optional, but an affirmative premise in the antecedent is necessary.

Rule 5—The conclusion always follows the weaker parts of the antecedent. This rule is more a corollary to the other four rules than a strict logical norm of validity for the categorical syllogistic. It is, in other words, rather a *guide* to a valid procedure; for it is a blending of some of the rudimentary axioms of the syllogistic and the logical rules already mentioned (e.g., invalidity of overdistribution in the conclusion: Rule 3). It lacks the independence of the other logical rules in the system. But it is helpful for it can often make one aware of some radical error in an argument or proof insofar as it is an application to logic of the adage, *A chain is no stronger than its weakest link.*

Rule 5 requires that the quality and quantity of the consequent of every valid categorical syllogism does not exceed the quality and quantity of the premises from which it was inferred. In other words, the sum total of the *weaknesses*, qualitatively and quantitatively, of the premises making up the antecedent should be evident in the valid consequent.

Of all categorical propositions, the *strongest* is the *A* proposition; the *weakest*, the *O* proposition. Between these limits all other propositions can be measured with a minimum of difficulty if we keep in mind (1) a negative premise is weaker than an affirmative premise in the order of *quality*, (2) a particular premise is weaker than a universal premise in the order of *quantity*, and (3) although an *E* premise is greater than an *I* premise in the order of *quantity*, the opposite is true in the order of *quality*. The following table perhaps makes these distinctions clearer.

In Quantity	*In Quality*
A and *E* are *mutually equal*	*A* and *I* are *mutually equal*
I and *O* are *weaker* than *A*	*E* and *O* are *weaker* than *A*
I and *O* are *weaker* than *E*	*E* and *O* are *weaker* than *I*
I and *O* are *mutually equal*	*E* and *O* are *mutually equal*

Aristotle did not explicitly state this fifth norm, but he certainly employed it in many illustrations concerning the logical value of syllogistic forms. For example: "If the middle term is related universally to one of the extremes, a particular negative syllogism must result whenever the middle term is related universally to the major whether positively or negatively, and particularly to the minor and in a manner opposite to that of the universal statement: *by an opposite manner* I mean, if the universal statement is negative, the particular is affirmative: if the universal is affirmative, the particular is negative. For if M belongs to no N, but to some O, it is necessary that N does not belong to some O."[15] In another place he states that "a universal statement is proved only when all the premises are universal."[16]

In practice, the fifth rule of the categorical syllogistic operates as follows: (1) When an *E* proposition and an *I* proposition appear in the antecedent of a categorical syllogism, the conclusion, to be *valid*, can be no stronger than an *O* proposition; (2) When an *A* proposition and an *O* proposition appear in the antecedent of a categorical syllogism, the conclusion, to be *valid*, can likewise be no stronger than an *O* proposition; and (3) When an *E* proposition and an *A* proposition appear simultaneously in the antecedent of a categorical syllogism, the conclusion, to be *valid*, can be no stronger than either an *E* or an *O* proposition.

Since there are four logical figures of the categorical syllogism, and each figure capable of sixteen moods, there are some 64 syllogistic forms that the categorical syllogism can take. But not all of these logical forms are *valid*. As we shall see in the Exercise section of this chapter there are at most only 24 syllogistic forms that observe all five of the logical canons for validity. Violation of even one of the logical rules invalidates a syllogistic form; and in fact seven moods in each of the four syllogistic figures (i.e., 28 syllogistic forms) are logically invalid because they evidently violate Rule 4.

II

Since Aristotle unequivocally considered the *first figure* the most excellent and most scientific figure of his categorical syllogistic, it is clearly understandable why the *reductive process* is more than just an integral part of his theory of the syllogism. His high regard for the first figure was based on its greater naturalness of thought sequence, its own perfection of logical rigor, and its own probative potentiality; it is the *only* syllogistic figure in which all four types of conclusion can be validly drawn, i.e., *A*, *E*, *I*, and *O*.[17] These four *perfect moods* appearing in the first figure have been traditionally labeled Barbar*a*, Celar*e*nt, Dar*ii*, Feri*o*. Within each Latin name are vowels that sequentially represent both the quality and quantity of each premise in these valid argument-forms. No other syllogistic figure can validly yield all four types of conclusion: in the *second* figure, all valid conclusions are *negative*; in the *third* figure, all valid conclusions are *particular*; and in the *fourth* figure, valid conclusions are normally *never universally affirmative*.

The Stagirite was well aware that the *valid imperfect moods* of his categorical syllogistic far outnumbered the *valid perfect moods*. Unlike the *perfect moods*, which he said "need nothing other than what has been stated to make plain what necessarily follows," Aristotle observes that all the valid syllogistic forms in the *second* and *third* logical figures are "imperfect," i.e., each "needs either one or more propositions, which are indeed the necessary consequences of the terms set down, but have not been expressly stated as premises."[18] In his unsophisticated axiomatization of the categorical syllogistic, the *perfect moods* of the first figure were to be employed as the fonts or matrices from which all the *valid imperfect moods* of the other figures would be derived and validated: "Finally, the first figure has no need of the others, while it is by means of the first that the other two figures are developed, and have their intervals close-packed until immediate premises are reached. Clearly, therefore, the first figure is the primary condition of knowledge."[19]

In this axiomatization, Aristotle's chief instrument was to be a logical procedure known as *reduction*. By this method all the valid syllogistic forms in the other three figures could be logically vindicated. The *reductive process* was to play an indispensable role in bringing to his theory of the categorical syllogism a desirable feature of every deductive system, viz., *completeness*. Reduction, then, is a logical procedure by which all the valid imperfect moods of the less perfect figures can be guaranteed in their validity in virtue of the first, and most perfect, figure. Reduction can be done either (a) *directly* or (b) *indirectly*, and Aristotle gives numerous instances of both types in his *Analytics*.

(a) The *direct method of reduction* to the perfect moods of the first figure consists almost entirely in some valid use of logical *conversion* as in the following example, where syllogism I, in the third figure, is directly reduced to syllogism II in the first figure.

> *Syll. I*   (If) no X is Y,
>
>   (and if) some X is Z,
>
>   (*then-therefore*) not all Z is Y.
>
> *Syll. II*   (If) no X is Y,
>
>   (and if) some Z is X,
>
>   (*then-therefore*) not all Z is Y.

This is a valid reduction to the first figure of an *E-I-O* mood syllogism in the third figure; since the middle-term of the major premise in syllogism I was already in the subject-term position, it needed no mutation at all. However, the logical law of *simple conversion* had to be employed to put the term-variable X in its proper place in the minor premise.

Sometimes, too, in the direct method of reduction the *transposing* of both premises may be necessary as can be seen in the following example.

> *Syll. I*
>
>   (If) all M is N,
>
>   (and if) no O is N,
>
>   (*then-therefore*) no O is M.

Syll. II

(If) no N is O,

(and if) all M is N,

(*then-therefore*) $\begin{cases} \text{no M is O;} \\ \text{no O is M.} \end{cases}$

This is a valid reduction to the first figure of an *A-E-E* mood syllogism in the second figure. *Transposition* of the premises of syllogism I was an added step necessary for a valid reduction to the first figure, since the standard *A* proposition converts only *accidentally* to an *I* proposition. After being transposed, the original minor premise, an *E* proposition, can be simply converted validly. Finally, the conclusion of the reduced syllogism ("no M is O") is then simply converted validly to the conclusion of the original syllogism ("no O is M").

(b) The *indirect method of reduction* to the perfect moods of the first figure is a much more complex operation than the direct method. It is likewise more challenging and more versatile, for it can be applied to *all* the valid imperfect moods in any of the other figures. Aristotle usually refers to this logical procedure as the *reduction to the impossible* in his theorizing about the syllogism in the *Analytics*. Basically, the indirect method consists in the valid use of two logical laws: *opposition* and *conversion*. The objective of this procedure is to show that, by virtue of the tremendous probative value of the perfect moods in the first figure, the *conclusion* or *consequent* of any valid syllogistic-form in the other figures cannot be denied with the same premises in its antecedent without some form of opposition, contrary or contradictory, inevitably resulting. Such a denial would imply, of course, that a logically bad or incorrect consequence can be present in a valid argument, which is *impossible*. The following syllogisms illustrate indirect reduction (note that the major and minor premises of syllogism I are accepted as *true*):

Syll. I

(If) no B is *A*,

(and if) some C is *A*,

(*then-therefore*) some C is not B.

Syll. II

(If) no *B* is A,

(and if) all C is *B*,

(*then-therefore*) no C is A.

If the *conclusion* of the original valid syllogism (syll. I), *some C is not B*, is denied despite its *true* premises, then, according to the basic principles of logical reasoning, its *contradictory* should be admitted: *all C is B* is its contradictory. And since the categorical proposition *no B is A* was previously accepted as a true premise, it can now be employed as the major premise in syllogism II; and *all C is B* will be employed as the minor premise in syllogism II. From these mutually acceptable premises the new conclusion is then validly drawn: *no C is A*. But this conclusion is the *contradictory* of a premise *some C is A* previously accepted as having a true truth-value in the original syllogism. Such a result shows the validity of the original syllogism.[20]

It should now be evident that the reasoning process involved in this *indirect method of reduction* has great affinity with the procedures commonly employed as proofs in the physical and mathematical sciences. Although it is a negative type of approach, the indirect method is a most effective one for vindicating *all* the imperfect moods that are logically valid. In short, the indirect method of reduction to the first figure is based on the axiom in logic *if a false conclusion follows from two or more true premises, then that which is not known to be true must be false and its contradictory true.*

III

In this section of the chapter we promised to consider the two major types of *informal* syllogistic argumentation: the *enthymeme* and the *sorites*. This is expedient because informality and brevity are two of the distinguishable characteristics of human discourse today. As masters of the art of rhetoric, successful advertisers, effervescent public-relations specialists, and popular speakers, know well how to let the *thymos* (the infrarational mind) of an audience supply what they purposely leave "unsaid." An effective speech is, one might say, a kind of dialogue between speaker and hearer; the speaker responds to what he can tell of his audience's reaction to what he is saying. Most of us are able to do this in ordinary conversation; in fact, rarely do we present our arguments in any formal syllogistic manner. We know that in contemporary society to say more than is polite or expedient, to make explicit what could be normally presupposed, and to assert or support our opinions in a highly formal way are unacceptable modes of social behavior. Still there are many occasions when formal argumentation is both expedient and necessary, notably in the academic world. The more important a subject appears, the more likely men will turn to formal discourse in their deliberations concerning it. Nevertheless, it is certainly true that the greater part of human discourse is ordered to informal, social ends.

Recognizing that men do not in their discourse commonly make use of syllogistic argument, Aristotle squarely faced the problem of the practical value of the categorical syllogistic; his *Rhetoric* treats of the dangers attending use of abridged arguments commonly known as *enthymemes*.[21] He there points out that those untrained in logic are easily misled or even victimized by their inability to detect fallacies lurking in the cool and shaded areas of the majority of abridged arguments. It is a fact that a person, incapable of unraveling or expanding enthymemic arguments into syllogistic form and depending mostly on guesswork as to their logical validity, is the defenseless prey of sophists anywhere. Therefore, some knowledge of the categorical syllogistic can be nothing but an advantage for anyone. Confronted with the disarming informality of an abbreviated syllogism, such as "All sinners are good, for nothing God-made is evil," a person trained in logic will recognize that a logical rule is here being cleverly trespassed or ignored; he remembers that the conclusion in a valid categorical syllogism must follow the weaker parts of its antecedent.

(a) The *enthymeme*, then, is a short-cut, a truncated way of syllogizing.[22] In Aristotle's day, however, "enthymeme" meant only those abridged syllogisms proceeding from probabilities or signs (e.g., This woman-suspect must be guilty, for she fainted during the cross-examination in the court trial). Nevertheless, regardless of its informal attire, the truncated syllogism has much in common with the more rigidly constructed categorical syllogism. Still, there is at least one principal difference that we should not overlook: in any such abridged argument at least one categorical proposition is omitted or "taken for granted," designedly or not.

Only on rare occasion is the *tacit*, unstated proposition the conclusion of the argument. Most frequently suppressed or omitted is the *major premise*, which is usually a universal categorical proposition: e.g.,

> (a) Since all men are animals, all men have empirical knowledge.
>
> (b) This chemical substance is an acid, because whenever it is applied to litmus paper, the paper turns blue.

In example (a) the universal categorical proposition "All animals are capable of empirical knowledge" is the presupposed major premise and would have to be supplied for construction of a valid syllogism in the first figure. Likewise, in example (b) the universal categorical proposition "Everything that turns litmus paper blue is an acid" is to be understood as the major premise in a valid syllogism of the first figure. Less frequently, the *minor premise* is left "unsaid" in an enthymeme: e.g., No ape is angelic, because nothing angelic is corporeal. In this example the categorical proposition "Every ape is corporeal" is the unexpressed minor premise in a valid syllogistic form of the second figure.

For the systematic analysis of enthymemic arguments, a few

general suggestions regarding procedure can be offered. (1) Every truncated syllogism should be measured immediately by the perfect moods of the first figure, since it is the only logical figure capable of all four types of conclusion (*A, E, I, O*); but the attempts at valid recasting should not end there except for the enthymeme that has an *A* conclusion. (2) The informality of the enthymeme does not exempt it from any of the rules of validity for the categorical syllogistic.[23] (3) In attempting to discover the real premise of an enthymeme one should look for some key word, such as *since, for,* or *because,* that designates the reason the conclusion is being drawn. (4) Normally the middle-term of the truncated argument will be found in that premise too. (5) Generally, the conclusion would be stated quite baldly and not be too difficult to identify.

(b) The *sorites* is also a form of syllogizing that omits propositions. It is an argument, however, that is less casual than an enthymeme; but it is usually much lengthier. A sorites is an argument in which categorical propositions are chained together in an orderly series, i.e., it is a form of polysyllogistic argumentation in which the term-extremes of relevant categorical propositions are designedly interlaced. In such *concatenated* syllogistic-forms, the conclusion of each separable categorical syllogism is normally left *tacit,* yet each individual syllogism is, so to speak, an indispensable link in the logical chain.

Traditionally, the sorites has been found in two classical forms: the Aristotelian (4th century B.C.), and the Goclenian (16th century A.D.). Each of these forms has its own distinctive and noticeable differences in logical structure. Yet there is one element shared by them: their ultimate conclusions are always composed of one of the *extremes* of the first categorical proposition in the series and one of the *extremes* of the categorical proposition that is the last premise in the argument. These conditions are essential to the validity of the logical procedure, yet each kind of soritical syllogizing will tend to satisfy these conditions in an unique manner. Of course, in this multi-proposition form of argument the logical rules for maintaining the identity of signification and supposition of the terms employed in all the premises must be observed.

(i) In the *Aristotelian sorites*[24] the argument consists of several categorical propositions syllogistically linked together in such a way that the predicate-term of the very first premise in the series, though it is actually the *minor* premise of the first syllogism, becomes the subject-term of the second premise; then, the predicate-term of the second premise becomes the subject-term of the third premise; and the same process continues until the *conclusion* is reached. The subject-term of the *conclusion* should be the subject-term of the first categorical proposition in the series; its predicate-term will be that of the last premise of the argument. An example of an Aristotelian sorites follows:

	Minor premise:	(If) *every M is N*,
Syllogism I	*Major premise*:	(and if) every N is O,
	Tacit conclusion:	(then-therefore) every M is O;
	Minor premise:	(and if) every O is P,
Syllogism II	*Major premise*:	(and if) every P is Q,
	Tacit conclusion:	(then-therefore) every O is Q;
	Minor premise:	(and if) every Q is R,
Syllogism III	*Major premise*:	(and if) every R is S,
	Tacit conclusion:	(then-therefore) every Q is S;
	Explicit conclusion:	(*then-therefore*) *every M is S.*

This type of sorites can be well illustrated also by a paraphrase of the famous argument by which G. Leibniz attempted to prove that the human soul is immortal:[25]

> (If) *every human soul* is a thinking substance,
> (and if) every thinking substance is immediately known simply,

(and if) everything immediately known simply is a thing whose activity does not contain parts,

(and if) everything whose activity does not contain parts is one whose activity is not motion,

(and if) everything whose activity is not motion is incorporeal,

(and if) every incorporeal substance is nonspatial,

(and if) every nonspatial substance is unsusceptible of motion,

(and if) everything unsusceptible of motion is indissoluble,

(and if) what is indissoluble is incorruptible,

(and if) what is incorruptible is *immortal,*

(*then-therefore*) *every human soul is immortal.*

Finally, it must be observed that in the valid Aristotelian sorites, only the first premise can be *particular*, and none of the premises except the last one can be *negative*. Otherwise an infraction of the syllogistic rule of validity disallowing *overdistribution* in the conclusion would result.

(ii) In the *Goclenian sorites* (named after Goclenius, 1547–1628) the argument is formulated from several categorical propositions syllogistically chained together in such a way that the subject-term of the first premise in the series (actually it is the *major* premise of the first syllogism too) becomes the predicate-term of the second premise; then the subject-term of the second premise becomes the predicate-term of the third premise; and the same process continues until the *conclusion* is reached. The subject-term of the *conclusion* should be the subject-term of the last premise of the argument; its predicate-term will be that of the first premise in the series. An example of a Goclenian sorites follows:

	Major premise:	(If) every D is *E*,
Syllogism I	*Minor premise*:	(and if) every C is D,
	Tacit conclusion:	(then-therefore) every C is E;

	Major premise:	(and if) every B is C,
Syllogism II	Minor premise:	(and if) *every A is B,*
	Tacit conclusion:	(then-therefore) every A is C;
	Explicit conclusion:	(*then-therefore*) *every A is E.*

This type of *sorites* may be illustrated also by the following argument, which attempts to prove that Stephen possesses immaterial images:

> (If) every knower *possesses immaterial images,*
>
> (and if) every animal is capable of being a knower,
>
> (and if) every man is an animal,
>
> (and if) *Stephen* is a man,
>
> (*then-therefore*) *Stephen possesses immaterial images.*

Finally, it must be observed that in the valid Goclenian sorites, only the first premise can be *negative*, and none of the premises except the last one can be *particular*. Otherwise one or more than one of the rules concerning *distribution* in valid forms of the categorical syllogistic would be violated.

This concludes our in-depth study of the categorical syllogistic. In the next two chapters we shall examine the *noncategorical syllogistic* from both the *traditional* and *nontraditional* points of view.

Pertinent Quotations about the validity of categorical syllogisms:

(a)

Of all the figures the most scientific is the first. Thus, it is the vehicle of the demonstrations of all the mathematical sciences, such as arithmetic, geometry, and optics, and practically of all sciences that investigate causes: for the syllogism of the reasoned fact is either exclusively or generally speaking and in most cases in this figure— a second proof that this figure is the most scientific; for grasp of a reasoned conclusion is the primary condition of knowledge. Thirdly, the first is the only figure which enables us to pursue knowledge of the essence of a thing. In the second figure no affirmative conclusion is possible, and knowledge of a thing's essence must be affirmative; while in the third figure the conclusion can be affirmative, but cannot be universal, and essence must have a universal character: e.g., man is not a two-footed animal in any qualified sense, but universally. Finally, the first figure has no need of the others, while it is by means of the first that the other two figures are developed, and have their intervals close-packed until immediate premises are reached. Clearly, therefore, the first figure is the primary condition of knowledge.

> —*The Basic Works of Aristotle*, tr. R. McKeon (New York: Random House, 1941), "Posterior Analytics I," ch. 14; by permission of the Clarendon Press, Oxford.

(b)

The power of *reducing* imperfect syllogisms to the perfect ones consists in this, that those syllogisms in which the regulative principles of syllogizing (the dictum de omni et nullo) are not so evidently or perfectly apparent, are reduced and proven through those in which such principles are perfectly and evidently preserved. Moreover, the most perfect modes of concluding are those first four of the first figure: Barbara, Celarent, Darii, and Ferio. For all conclusions capable of being inferred are some one of these (i.e., *A, E, I, O*). . . . Therefore, all these other moods, concluding either directly or indirectly, can be reduced to these four, and through them be proved. And reduction is two-fold: one is ostensive, the other is per impossible. The ostensive way employs two principles, namely, that of conversion and that of transportation, as the major premise is changed with the minor, or the minor is changed with the major.

> —John of St. Thomas, *Cursus phil. Thomisticus*, "Logica," part I, bk. III, ch. 7 (author's translation).

(c)

I call the *enthymeme* a rhetorical syllogism, and the example a rhetorical induction. Everyone who effects persuasion through proof does in fact use either enthymemes or examples. There is no other way.

> —*The Basic Works of Aristotle*, tr. R. McKeon (New York: Random House, 1941), "Rhetoric I," ch. 2; by permission of the Clarendon Press, Oxford.

(d)

The *enthymeme* is an imperfect syllogism, i.e., a composite expression in which, some propositions being presupposed, a hurried conclusion is drawn, as "every animal runs, therefore every man runs." In this argument, the proposition "Every man is an animal" is lacking; if it had been expressed, there would be a syllogism. It must be understood that every enthymeme should be reduced to a syllogistic form. This is so, for in any enthymeme there are three terms, as in any syllogism, two of which are placed in the conclusion. These are the *extremes*; and that which is not found in the conclusion is the *middle term*.

> —Peter of Spain (Pope John XXI), *Summulae Logicales*, bk. VII, tract V (Marietti edit.) (author's translation) p. 45.

Exercise:

(I) Check the *validity* of the categorical syllogisms in the previous chapter's exercise. If an argument is found to be *invalid*, state the most obvious rule that is broken.

(2) Work out the logical value of each of the other 36 syllogistic forms not invalidated by Rule 4 as shown by the asterisk in the conclusion, then apply the other four rules to determine whether the nine syllogistic forms for each figure are valid or invalid. State a logical reason for your decision.

Figure I

Major premise:	A	A	A	A		E	E	E	E		I	I	I	I		O O O O
Minor premise:	A	E	I	O		A	E	I	O		A	E	I	O		A E I O
			*				*					*	*			* * *
Conclusion:	. . . .					. . . .					. . . .					. . . .

Figure II

Major premise:	A	A	A	A		E	E	E	E		I	I	I	I		O O O O
Minor premise:	A	E	I	O		A	E	I	O		A	E	I	O		A E I O
			*				*					*	*			. * * *
Conclusion:	. . . .					. . . .					. . . .					. . . .

Figure III

Major premise:	A	A	A	A		E	E	E	E		I	I	I	I		O O O O
Minor premise:	A	E	I	O		A	E	I	O		A	E	I	O		A E I O
			*				*					*	*			* * *
Conclusion:	. . . .					. . . .					. . . .					. . . .

Figure IV

Major premise:	A	A	A	A		E	E	E	E		I	I	I	I		O O O O
Minor premise:	A	E	I	O		A	E	I	O		A	E	I	O		A E I O

		*	*		* *	* * *

Conclusion: . . . .

(3) Change these *truncated and concatenated* syllogisms into standardized forms so as to test their logical value. If any are found to be *invalid*, state the most obvious rule that is broken:

(a) All men are good drivers, because no women are men.

(b) Since every M is O, every O is N.

(c) Not everyone who cries "Lord, Lord" will enter the kingdom of heaven, for no faker will enter the kingdom of heaven.

(d) He must be untrustworthy, for he refuses to look anyone squarely in the eye.

(e) (If) all my sisters are slim,

(and if) none of my sisters is healthy,

(and if) all the intemperate members of my family are obese,

(and if) none of my brothers is unhealthy,

(*then-therefore*) all my sisters are unhealthy.

(f) (If) everything corporeal is a substance,

(and if) everything living is corporeal,

(and if) every plant is living,

(and if) every rose is a plant,

(*then-therefore*) every rose is a substance.

(g) (If) some angels are saints,

(and if) all saints are perfectly happy,

(and if) all perfectly happy beings are actually seeing God,

(and if) no one actually seeing God is in hell,

(*then-therefore*) some angels are not in hell.

9

The Noncategorical
Syllogistic
(traditional presentation)

A fairly good acquaintance with the main features of the categorical syllogistic should prove helpful as we are now introduced
to the noncategorical form of the syllogistic, for many similarities
exist between them: e.g., their inferential feature and their logical
purpose. Still this separate examination of the noncategorical
syllogistic is needed, because the two syllogistics are extremes in
the same genus and do have some polar differences. These differences we shall see are derived from their peculiar logical structure
and their proper norms for validity.

The noncategorical syllogistic (sometimes called *hypothetical*
or *compound*) has distinctive features that deserve a rather
thorough analysis. This analysis is intended to be carried on from
two different, but related, points of view or approaches that are
known as the *traditional approach* and the *nontraditional* or
modern approach. Each approach has been praised by scholarly
logicians for its own contributions to this part of logic. The main
objective, then, of this chapter will be to examine the chief and
distinctive features of the *traditional approach* to the noncategorical syllogistic; in the next chapter the salient and proper

features of the *nontraditional approach* to the noncategorical syllogistic will be examined.

It will be recalled that a close relationship obtains between the *propositional terms* (major and minor extremes in reference to the middle-term) of all standardized categorical syllogisms. This characteristic will be found lacking in the formulation of the noncategorical syllogism. But in lieu of a close connection between propositional terms, there is in the noncategorical syllogistic a formal connection between the *propositions themselves* that make up its antecedent and consequent. This difference is considered to be a fundamental one by logicians and is a radical reason for the emergence of the two sets of proximate logical standards for deciding on the probative value of arguments cast in dissimilar syllogistic forms.

Since any noncategorical syllogism is generally composed of *at least one noncategorical proposition* in its antecedent, one will find it helpful to review the chapter in this book that explained the more common forms of noncategorical statements: conditional or material implication; disjunctive or alternation; and, conjunctive. Because all noncategorical propositions are reducible to one of these classes, regardless of their peculiar structure (e.g., exponibles), each noncategorical proposition is a perfect composite truth-value statement that meaningfully signifies at least two mental judgments. In its conventional dress, the noncategorical statement is easily recognizable, openly appearing as a logical unit of two or more atomic or categorical propositions linked together by a sentential connective, such as "either, or" or "if, then" (e.g., *if* you ask the Father for anything in my name, *then* He will give it to you).

The noncategorical syllogism has a relatively standardized form: i.e., its major premise is a noncategorical proposition; its minor premise and its conclusion are usually categorical propositions. Both the categorical propositions in this kind of syllogistic are to be in some way relevant *operationally* to the major premise (i.e., by positing or denying its parts). The special type or class of noncategorical syllogistic is chiefly determined by the kind of noncategorical proposition that appears as the major premise: e.g.,

> If (Communists are deceivers), then (they are immoral).
>
> But, it is an undeniable fact that (Communists are deceivers).
>
> Therefore, (they are immoral).

In the example above, which is a logically valid syllogistic form, the minor premise posits or affirms one part (antecedent) of the syllogism's major premise insofar as it restates it substantially. Besides, it is not less evident in the example that the other part (consequent) of the major premise is denied or destroyed in the conclusion. This is what is meant by the expression *operational relevance* that should obtain between the propositions in the noncategorical syllogistic. Without such relevance, an argument would be meaningless. Standard operational procedures, too, are as necessary for correct argumentation as they are for any other successful human activity, e.g., the safe landing of an aircraft. We shall see that indiscriminate positings and denials by the minor premise and the conclusion in this syllogistic form are infractions of logically sound rules of reasoning.

Since the more common forms of the noncategorical syllogistic are the *conditional* type and the *disjunctive* type, and since all others can ultimately be reducible to these two types, they will receive a more detailed examination. Whereas the *conjunctive* type of the noncategorical syllogistic deserves less consideration because of its real or apparent lack of implicational potential.

I

Of the noncategorical or hypothetical forms of the syllogistic, the *conditional* is most frequently used. Without doubt this popular use of the conditional syllogism by men occurs because the human mind consistently exhibits a natural inclination to draw out implications or inferences from most statements. This tendency to see other statements within a statement is definitely an ability we humans are aware we possess to some degree.

Appearing as the major premise of the standardized non-categorical syllogism, the conditional proposition is essentially composed of two parts, technically known as the *antecedent* and the *consequent*. The *antecedent* contains the conditioned factor of the statement and usually appears first, but not necessarily: e.g., "I would have bought you the ticket had I known you wanted to attend the concert." However, since the antecedent normally has a priority of position in the statement and is preceded by the particle *if*, or an equivalent word, it is easily identifiable: e.g., "If the Congo's deeply-rooted social problems will be solved, then political unity will prevail in central Africa." On the other hand, the *consequent* is the statement that generally signifies what results or does not result from the fulfillment or the nonfulfillment of the earlier condition or conditions. The consequent, as seen in the last example, will normally be preceded by the particle *then*, or an equivalent word, that designates an illation or inference is involved.

Besides having a conditional proposition for its major premise, the conditional syllogistic will need to have its minor premise and its conclusion made up of categorical propositions that *logically operate* on the statements contained in the major premise, i.e., by affirming or denying the antecedent and/or the consequent: e.g.,

> If (the students have colds), then (they need quinine);
>
> But (the students do have colds);
>
> Therefore, (they need quinine).

> If (cats are vertebrates), then (they have hearts);
>
> But (cats do not have hearts),
>
> Therefore, (they are not vertebrates).

Unless these general notions proper to the conditional syllogistic are evident, arguments should be treated according to the categorical syllogistic forms to which they are easily reducible: e.g.,

> *Syll. I*:   If M is, then N is;
>
>   But, if O is, then M is;
>
>   Therefore, if O is, then N is.

> *Syll. II*:   (If) all M is N,
>
>   (and if) all O is M,
>
>   (*then-therefore*) all O is N.

Prior to examining the *validity* factors of the conditional syllogistic one should be somewhat informed of its controversial nature. Logicians have disputed about the nature of the conditional syllogism principally because they differed in their theories about *meaning* and *truth*.[1] For most Aristotelians, as we indicated earlier in this book, categorical and noncategorical propositions employed in valid syllogizing are expected to have some grounding in objective being and be causally related: e.g., "If children fool with fire, then they can be burned." For many logicians with other philosophical commitments, *meaningfulness* of conditional statements does not need such ontic grounding: e.g., "If the U.S.A. loses its poise in Vietnam, then it is raining out." Such logicians think that any *causal* dependence other than that conceived by Hume is not to be looked for in the conditional proposition or the conditional syllogism. The Stoics are usually credited with introducing this form of conditionalizing; it is not a novel creation.[2] In modern logic it is known as *material implication*. That material implications are as logically formal illations as conditionals in which there is some causal relevance is denied by most Aristotelians (texts exposing this controversy can be read at the end of this chapter).[3]

It has been the experience of most people to recognize that not every conditional argument is logically valid. Ordinarily, this defect in reasoning comes about from some logically-incorrect operational procedure involving the minor premise and/or the consequent in their relationship with the major premise of the noncategorical syllogism. Although each of the atomic or categorical propositions employed in the noncategorical syllogistic can posit (affirm) or destroy (deny) one or more of the parts of the major premise, still the choice of each to proceed validly is limited. Likewise the sequence of functions engaged in by the minor premise and the consequent in the conditional syllogistic affects its validity. Caution in this regard will be sufficient if one remembers that the KEY to every valid operation involving conditional syllogisms is primarily associated with the functions of the minor premise; the conclusion should follow its direction.

To function *validly*, then, the minor premise of the conditional syllogism will *posit*, i.e., *affirm*, in a special way; or else it will *destroy*, i.e., *deny*, in a special way. Otherwise, the logical form of such a noncategorical syllogism will inevitably be defective, principally because there has been a violation of some basic norm of logical reasoning. Aristotle offers an example of a violation of this kind, the fallacy of affirming the consequent: "When two things are so related to each other, that if the one is, the other by necessity is, then if the latter is not, the former will not be either; but if the latter is, it is not necessary that the former should be."[4] Every valid conditional syllogistic form will observe these two logical canons.

(a) *If the minor premise posits or affirms*, then it must do so to the antecedent of the major premise, and the conclusion will do the same to the consequent of the major premise: e.g.,

         (ant.)   (cons.)
If M is N, then O is P;

But M is N;   (ant. identically restated)

Therefore, O is P.   (cons. identically restated)

         (ant.)   (cons.)
If M is not N, then O is not P;

But M is not N;   (ant. identically restated)

Therefore, O is not P. (cons. identically restated)

(b) *If the minor premise destroys or denies*, then it must do so to the consequent of the major premise, and the conclusion will do the same to the antecedent of the major premise: e.g.,

    (ant.)   (cons.)

If M is N, then O is P;

But O is not P;   (cons. is denied or destroyed)

Therefore, M is not N.   (ant. is denied or destroyed)

    (ant.)   (cons.)

If M is not N, then O is not P;

But O is P;   (cons. is denied or destroyed)

Therefore, M is N.   (ant. is denied or destroyed)

These two logical rules concerning the *validity* of noncategorical conditional syllogisms need some further explanation. It is simply asserted in (a) that to infer conversely the fulfillment of any of the many possible or specific conditions in the antecedent is a logically defective procedure, for there would be neither a real nor logical assurance that one condition depended on the other: e.g., "If I fall asleep (go to the cinema, watch TV, etc.), then I will flunk the semester examination; but I did flunk the semester examination; therefore, I fell asleep etc." Both the traditional and nontraditional schools of logic are in substantive agreement with the logical soundness of this law that invalidates such argument forms. This logical law is commonly known as the *modus ponens*.

Whereas it is simply asserted in (b) that the nonfulfillment of the consequent of the major premise reasonably allows for the inference of any one or even all of its possible conditions in the antecedent, insofar as the consequent *did not de facto occur* and none of the alleged conditions which would bring about the consequent were fulfilled: e.g., "If I overeat, then I shall get sick; but de facto I did not get sick; therefore, I did not overeat." The logical soundness of this law as a validating principle in inferential reasoning is likewise agreed on substantively by both the traditional and nontraditional schools of logic. This logical law is commonly known as the *modus tollens*. In the next chapter these two logical laws will be shown by the truth-table method to be logically valid.

II

Like any noncategorical syllogistic, the standardized *disjunctive* syllogism has a special kind of noncategorical proposition, i.e., a disjunctive, as its major premise, and both its minor premise and its conclusion are categorical propositions. From our previous study we should recall that a *disjunctive* proposition is made up of two or more categorical truth-value statements joined together by the special sentential connective *either, or*: e.g., "*Either* Russian ships approaching Cuba would submit to search by the U.S. Navy, *or* President Kennedy promised they would be sunk." The logical unity needed in this type of noncategorical syllogistic will be guaranteed, like the conditional type, only if its minor premise and its conclusion will be operationally related to what is designated by the propositions constituting the major premise.

However, unlike the conditional syllogistic, no orderly sequence of logical operations is to be rigorously followed for validity. Regardless of the kind of opposition that exists between the statements in the major premise, the valid way of proceeding logically is as follows: if one part of the major premise is *affirmed* in the minor premise, then the other part(s) should be denied in the conclusion; and if one part of the major premise is *denied* in the minor premise, then the other part(s) should be affirmed in the conclusion. Perhaps two examples will help clarify this procedure:

> Either Helen passes the final exam, or she flunks for the semester.
>
> But Helen does pass the final exam.   (affirmation)
>
> Therefore, Helen does not flunk for the semester. (denial)

> Either Marge passes the final exam, or she flunks for the semester.
>
> But Marge does not pass the final exam.   (denial)
>
> Therefore, Marge does flunk for the semester.   (affirmation)

That there are two distinctive types of disjunction is not a discovery of modern logicians; they were known even as far back as the Megarian-Stoic era.[5] These two types of disjunctive syllogisms are called *exclusive* and *nonexclusive*.

(a) The *exclusive* or *strict* disjunctive syllogism is one in which the major premise asserts that one and only one of the two or more propositional statements (called *disjuncts*) is *true*, because there is a mutual incompatibility between them. Another way of saying this is that at least one but only one of the propositions in the major premise has a true truth-value: e.g., "Either you will pass this final examination, or you will fail for the semester." In this strict or pure disjunction there is no in-between.

(b) The *nonexclusive* or *weak* disjunctive syllogism is by far the more popularly employed type of disjunction. Its major premise will usually contain an incomplete list of *alternative* propositions (called *alternates*), *one of which at least will be true*. It happens often that two or more of the alternates have a true truth-value: e.g., The bishop will either fly from Chicago to New York, or take a train, or go by bus, or even cycle." Sometimes this type of syllogistic is referred to as *alternation* rather than disjunction; traditionally it was known as the "quasi-disjunctive syllogism."[6]

The nonexclusive disjunctive syllogistic is quite standardized as to its valid operational procedure of positing and destroying what is asserted in the major premise. In this weak kind of disjunction, the affirmation of an alternate does not necessitate an outright denial of all the other alternates: e.g., "Either the cross-country varsity team won, or it lost the race; but it did not win the race; therefore, it lost the race." Such a conclusion would be logically invalid if it was factually untrue. In other words, this type of disjunction does hinge on a sufficient enumeration of possibilities or alternates, for in the last example there might have been a *tie*. Hence, the logically proper sequence to follow in the quasi-disjunctive syllogistic is for the minor premise first to deny one part of the major premise, and then for the conclusion to posit or affirm the other part or parts: e.g., "Lloyd is going to join either the Army, or Navy, or Marines, or Air Force, or Coast Guard; but he did not join the Marines; therefore, Lloyd is either in the Army, Navy, Air Force, or Coast Guard."

III

Before concluding this chapter a brief treatment of the *conjunctive* or *copulative* syllogistic will be given. As the least common of noncategorical syllogisms, the conjunctive syllogistic usually has its major premise structured from two or more atomic statements joined together in a logical unit by such distinctive sentential connectives as *and*, *but*, or *moreover*: e.g., "John Kennedy was assassinated *and* Johnson took the oath of office in the airplane." The conjunctive syllogism has categorical propositions as its minor premise and its conclusion, and they will be related to the major premise in content-matter and operationally, i.e., by either positing or destroying, or both.

In the valid conjunctive syllogistic, however, only the positing or affirming of those propositions constituting the major premise is logically permissible, for if a conjunctive proposition taken as a whole is to have a true truth-value then all its parts must have a true truth-value. The traditional and nontraditional schools of logic are in perfect concord on this point, as will be seen in the next chapter.

Whatever *implicational* potential is contained in a conjunctive syllogism tends to become more apparent when it is recast into one or other of the more common types of noncategorical syllogistic. Nevertheless, after such recastings the validity of the syllogistic is still regulated by the norms proper to the syllogistic form used: e.g.,

> (original): John Kennedy was assassinated and Johnson took the oath of office in the airplane.

> (recast): It is false that either John Kennedy was not assassinated, or that Johnson took the oath of office in the airplane. (N.B. it is *false* that either disjunct is false).

Thus we conclude the traditional presentation of the non-categorical or compound syllogistic. That such a presentation can be complemented and perfected by some formal factors contributed by the nontraditional school of logic will be shown in the following chapter.

Pertinent Quotations about the noncategorical syllogistic:

(a)

In general whenever A and B are such that they cannot belong at the same time to the same thing, and one of the two necessarily belongs to everything, and again C and D are related in the same way, and A follows C but the relation cannot be reversed, then D must follow B and the relation cannot be reversed. And A and D may belong to the same thing, but B and C cannot. First it is clear from the following consideration that D follows B. For since either C or D necessarily belongs to everything; and since C cannot belong to that to which B belongs, because it carries A along with it and A and B cannot belong to the same thing; it is clear that D must follow B. Again since C does not reciprocate with A, but C or D belongs to everything, it is possible that A and D should belong to the same thing. But B and C cannot belong to the same thing, because A follows C; and so something impossible results. It is clear then that

B does not reciprocate with D either, since it is possible that D and A should belong at the same time to the same thing.

> —*The Basic Works of Aristotle*, tr. R. McKeon (New York: Random House, 1941), "Prior Analytics I," ch. 46; and also see comments of Fr. Bochenski in *ibid.*, pp. 95–96; by permission of the Clarendon Press, Oxford.

(b)

For as every disjunctive is true if (and only if) it contains a true (proposition) and since one of (two contradictorily) opposed (propositions) is evidently always true, it must certainly be said that the (proposition) so formed is true.

> —Sextus Empiricus, *Adversus Mathematicos* Vol. 8, p. 282 (quoted in *ibid.*, I. M. Bochenski, p. 119).

(c)

In regulating the goodness of any sort of consequence one most universal principle is offered, from which the rest are derived, and to which they are reduced, namely: in a good consequence the antecedent cannot be given as true and the consequent false; but if the antecedent is true, so too the consequent. This principle is immediately reducible to that most supreme of principles: any thing either is or is not; or, it is impossible for the very same entity simultaneously to be and not to be. For if the antecedent is true, it is already signified as such; moreover, if the consequent is false, it drags along after itself its antecedent by reason of the connection which the truth of the consequent has with the truth of the antecedent: it is, therefore, the same to place the true antecedent and false consequent as to place the antecedent as true and partly false, because the consequent is, as it were, a special part and something of the antecedent, if it truly is something connected with it, and the consequence is that very connection. That which, however, is partly false is not absolutely true, therefore, if the antecedent is given as true and the consequent false . . . then the antecedent is given as true and non-true, which are contradictory.

—John of St. Thomas, *Cursus Phil. Thomisticus*, "Logica," part I, bk. III, ch. 11 (author's translation) p. 67.

(d)

It follows concerning the hypothetical proposition. It is that type of proposition which has two categoricals as their own subordinate principal parts, as "if man runs, man is moved." And it is called "hypothetical" from the word "hypos" which is "under" and "thesis" —"position," as if "suppositive," because one part is placed under the other. Of hypothetical propositions, one is conditional, another is copulative, still another is disjunctive. The CONDITIONAL is that in which two categoricals are joined together through this copula "if," as "if man runs, man is moved"; and that categorical proposition, to which is immediately united the connective "if" is called the antecedent; the other, truly, is the consequent. The COPULATIVE is that in which two categoricals are joined together through this copula "and," as "Socrates runs, *and* Plato disputes." The DISJUNCTIVE is that in which two categoricals are joined together through this copula "or," as "Socrates runs, *or* Plato disputes."

For the Conditional to be true it is exigent that the antecedent not be able to be true without the consequent, as "if man is, animal is"; whence every true Conditional is necessary, and every false Conditional is impossible. For its falsity, it suffices that the antecedent may be true without a true consequent, as "if man is, then he is white." For the truth of the Copulative it is necessary that both parts be true, as "God exists, *and* Man is an animal." For its falsity, it is sufficient that one part be false, as "Man is an animal, *and* a horse is a stone." For the truth of the Disjunctive it suffices that one part be true, as "man is an animal *or* a raven is a stone" and it is permissible that both parts of it be true, but not so properly, as "man is an animal *or* a horse is capable of whinnying." For its falsity it is sufficient that both parts be false, as "man is not an animal, *or* a horse is a stone."

—Peter of Spain (Pope John XXI), *Summulae Logicales*, tract I, (Marietti edit.) (author's translation) pp. 7–8.

Exercise:

Indicate in the spaces provided the logical evaluation of these non-categorical syllogisms:

     (a) If M is O, then N is P

         @ M is O

         Therefore: N is P   . . . .

     (b) If M is O, then N is not P

         @ M is O

         Therefore: N is not P   . . . .

     (c) Either M is not O, or N is P

         @ N is not P

         Therefore: M is O   . . . .

     (d) If M is not O, then N is P

         @ M is not O

         Therefore: N is P   . . . .

     (e) If M is not O, then N is not P

         @ M is not O

         Therefore: N is not P   . . . .

     (f) If M is not O, then N is not P

         @ N is not P

Therefore: M is O   . . . .

(g) If M is not O, then N is P

@ N is not P

Therefore: M is not O   . . . .

(h) If M is O, then N is not P

@ N is P

Therefore: M is not O   . . . .

(i) If M is not O, then N is P

@ N is not P

Therefore: M is O   . . . .

(j) Either M is O, or N is not P

@ M is not O

Therefore: N is P   . . . .

(k) If M is not O, then N is not P

@ N is P

Therefore: M is not O   . . . .

(l) Either M is not O, or N is not P

@ M is not O

Therefore: N is P   . . . .

10

The Noncategorical
Syllogistic
(nontraditional presentation)

Since noncategorical arguments are a special concern of non-traditional logicians, the primary objective of this chapter is to introduce the student to some of the common techniques employed by nontraditional logicians in appraising the logical value of noncategorical arguments. Such an introduction requires that one becomes acquainted with the background of nontraditional logic or the "new logic," as it is sometimes called. No logician denies that traditional and nontraditional are two different kinds of logic, nevertheless they both have some salient similarities. In order to achieve this primary goal, then, there will be four sections in this chapter: (1) an introduction to the names of the "new logic" that is nontraditional, and an examination of both its reasons for coming into being and its growth to the present time; (2) an analysis of its distinctive features as a propositional calculus; (3) an examination of the interdefinability of its truth-table functions; and (4) a formal consideration of some techniques it uses commonly to appraise the validity of noncategorical arguments.

I

Since the turn of this century nontraditional logic has far out-
stripped the other kinds of logic (e.g., traditional and Indian)
in popularity and prestige. This fact cannot be honestly denied
by any unjaundiced logician. It has enjoyed a tremendous appeal
to specialists in many fields of learning over the last seventy
years. Because of its distinctive "new look," nontraditional logic
has been given many new names, such as "theoretical logic,"
"mathematical logic," "modern logic," and "symbolic logic."

From the point of view of *meaning*, the last name, *symbolic
logic*, is least suitable because all logics are dependent on signs
or symbols, i.e., on entities that represent something other than
themselves to a knowing power. Nevertheless, since this type of
logic tends so strongly to the use of ideographic signifiers (those
standing for concepts and/or judgments) rather than to the
more common phonographic signifiers, i.e., words such as *hat*
and *coat* employed in everyday conversations, it is aptly named
"symbolic logic."

But this novel brand of logic is more suitably called "mathematical logic" because it has three distinctive characteristics:
(a) it is constructed along the lines of a calculus that stresses
formalism as a general principle of its logical methodology;
(b) it attempts constantly to devise better logical systems of
reasoning in order to obtain greater exactness and rigor in argumentation; (c) it tends to formulate its own basic logical laws,
axioms, and theorems in a language that is made of arbitrarily-
designated signifiers (called an *object language*) that are known
as *variables, constants* or *functors*, and *quantifiers*. A fuller
understanding of these features will develop as this chapter un-
folds.

The reasons often given for the existence of nontraditional logic
are multiple; however, only those reasons that are directly pertinent to logic itself are of immediate interest to us now. Since the
validity of arguments is the chief concern of the logician, he is
more interested in their "form" or "structure" than in their
content-matter. The designed detachment from interest in the

matter of arguments is best ensured according to nontraditional logicians by creating new kinds of "scientific language." Equipped with technical media that resemble greatly the equations and formulas found so often in the sciences of chemistry and mathematics, nontraditional logicians contend that arguments or proofs would be given greater probative value and many of the handicaps to more rigorous reasoning would be minimized (e.g., solecisms, equivocations, and other forms of ambiguity). Besides, the deceptions that arise from rhetoric and emotionalism, so inherent in languages employing verbal signifiers exclusively, could be more easily detected.

These creators of such scientific languages claim also that there would be greater, even global, comprehensibility about them as there is in a sheet of musical notes, and that a scientific language offers to the logicians an operational maneuverability in the sphere of argumentation or proofs that surpasses· "natural languages" as do Arabic numerals the Roman numerals in mathematics: e.g., 20×20, and $XX \times XX$. Translating the arguments of everyday social intercourse and those of the academic world into a scientific code or shorthand would then make the testing of their logical value an easy and efficient operation. Contemporary nontraditional logicians are quite in agreement that all these reasons have been justified; actually traditional logicians have little basis for quarrelling on this score.

That nontraditional or modern logic makes almost total use of ideographic signifiers in its various deductive systems is a fact. But in no way must this be looked upon as a totally original creation in logic, for this type of nonverbal signifier was unknown either to the ancient Hellenic logicians or to the logicians of the Middle Ages. As a matter of fact, the historians of logic agree unanimously that there was only a limited use of ideographic designators in the domain of logic till 1666, when G. Leibniz (1646–1716) wrote his scholarly work, *De Arte Combinatoria*. Leibniz is now rightly acclaimed the "founder" and "originator" of the newly developed or nontraditional logic.

There was still another factor that played a considerable role in conditioning the growth of nontraditional or mathematical logic: the centuries old dissatisfaction with the Euclidean system. This chronic disenchantment had bothered mathematicians for centuries and crystallized in the middle of the nineteenth century with the creation of non-Euclidean geometries by Nicolai Lobachevsky, a Russian mathematician, and Bernard Riemann, a German mathematician.[1] About the same time nontraditional logic was also becoming of age with the famous publications of George Boole (1815–1864).[2] Some of the greatest contributors to the growth of nontraditional logic since then have been De Morgan, Peirce, Frege, Hilbert, Peano, Russell, Whitehead, Lukasiewicz, Carnap, Tarski, Godel, Bochenski, Thomas and Church.[3]

II

That nontraditional logic is essentially a *propositional calculus* is evident not only from what we have seen of its mathematical lineage but also from the major factors that constitute it: *variables* and *constants*. *Variables* are ideographic symbols used by modern logicians to designate both classes of things and propositions, usually categorical ones. *Constants* or *functors* are ideographic symbols used by modern logicians to designate some type of logical operation, like implication or disjunction.

(a) *Variables* are considered by nontraditional logicians to be of two general types: (1) *term variables*, and (2) *propositional variables*. *Term variables* are used in statements as signifiers that designate things, classes, and ideas. In many systems of nontraditional logic the notations for term variables are capital letters like "A," "B," and "C": e.g., the categorical proposition "All apples are bad" may be written symbolically as "All A are B" by substituting the term variables A for "apples" and B for "bad." A cursory look at the *Analytics* will show that although Aristotle was well aware of the use of term variables in logic, he did not seem to have an awareness of the advantages of extending the notion of "variable" to statements as a whole. The Stoics are credited for this insight, and it was an innovation that was to advance the growth of logic.

Propositional variables are generally employed by nontraditional logicians as signifiers to designate the categorical propositions that constitute a noncategorical or compound statement. In many systems of nontraditional logic the notations for propositional variables are small letters like "p," "q," "r," "s," and "t," and are used in place of any simple or atomic proposition involved in a logical operation. Substituting such propositional variables for the antecedent and consequent of a conditional proposition like "If Kenya is a new republic, then more Africans are free," it would be symbolized logically according to one system "If p then q." We shall see soon that the sentential connective *if then* also has its own distinctive symbolization. Another example is the symbolization that occurs in a disjunctive proposition like "Either the prince will marry, or the kingdom's weal is in jeopardy." Substituting such propositional variables for the alternates of this disjunctive proposition it would be symbolized logically according to one system "Either r or s." The sentential connective *either-or* likewise has its own distinctive symbolization. It should now be evident that in all such instances the categorical propositions that make up compound or noncategorical statements can be represented adequately by propositional variables.

(b) *Constants* or *functors* in nontraditional logic make the symbolization of noncategorical statements complete, for they are usually employed to represent sentential connectives that designate a variety of logical operations in which propositional variables are involved. Logical constants are in some ways like the operational symbols employed in arithmetic, for example the plus sign, "+," that indicates the additional operation: e.g., $2 + 2 = 4$. But unlike the commonly known arithmetic symbols for arithmetical functions which are represented in the same way universally, sentential connectives are variously symbolized in nontraditional logic.[4] As a result one has to know the logical system (for each has its own systematic notation) to be able to evaluate the argument or proof. This situation is a major handicap, for not seldom a notational system in nontraditional logic can be as meaningless as a foreign language is to one not acquainted with it. Leibniz's dream of a logical language that would be universally meaningful is still unrealized.

Principally for the sake of convenience the simple notations of Peano-Russell-Whitehead will be employed in this chapter.[5] We shall consider *six* of the most commonly used constants or functors that designate a distinct logical operation. (1) The tilde is a constant that represents a negation or *contradictory function*. Written "∼", it is only placed before a propositional variable or a group of propositional variables (e.g., "∼p," "∼(p · q)") and is translated as *it is not the case that* or *it is false that*. (2) The dot is a constant that designates the *conjunctive function*. Written " · ", it is always placed between two or more propositional variables or even groups of propositional variables (e.g., "p · q," "p · (q · r)") and is translated as *and* or *but* or some equivalent expression. (3) The wedge is a constant that signifies the weak *disjunctive function*. Written "∨," it is always placed between two or more propositional variables or even groups of propositional variables (e.g., "p ∨ q," "p ∨ q ∨ (∼p ∨ r)") and is translated as *either-or* or some equivalent expression. (4) The inverted wedge is a constant that designates the strong disjunctive function (alternation). Written " ∧", it too is always placed between two or more propositional variables or even groups of propositional variables (e.g., "p ∧ q," "p ∧ (∼q · r)") and is translated also as *either-or*. (5) The horseshoe is a constant that signifies about any sort of a *conditional function*. Written "⊃", it is likewise always placed between two or more propositional variables or even groups of propositional variables (e.g., "p ⊃ q," "p ⊃ (q ∨ r)") and is translated as *if then* or some equivalent expression. In nontraditional logic this functor symbolizes what is called "material implication." (6) Having no definite name, the symbol "≡" designates the *biconditional function* and is always placed between two or more propositional variables or even groups of propositional variables (e.g., "p ≡ q," "p ≡ (∼q ∨ r)") and is translated as *if and only if* or some equivalent expression. In nontraditional logic this constant or sentential connective symbolizes what is called "material equivalence."

Prior to examining each of these constants or functors further a few remarks about the *scope* of a constant or functor might be helpful. The scope of a functor is the extent of influence it exerts on the propositional variable or propositional variables with which it is involved. The scope of the tilde is said to be unilateral because it extends only in one direction, i.e., to the propositional variable or propositional variables which follow it (e.g., "~p"). It is the most primitive of the logical operations for no logical system can be formulated without a negating functor. The other five constants or functors are called *binary* or *dyadic* insofar as the scope of each is bilateral, i.e., its influence extends to what precedes it and to what follows it in the whole statement. In short, binary functors are meant to express a relational operation *between* at least two or more propositional variables (e.g., "p ∨ q").

To understand the *definitions* of each of these six constants or functors which are to follow, we should remember that every proposition, categorical and noncategorical, is essentially a truth-value statement; it is either *true* or it is *false*. As was pointed out earlier, nontraditional logicians are not unanimously agreed on the nature of *truth*. But even those who think that truth and falsity are mere logical values arbitrarily assigned to propositions or propositional variables for more efficient logical operations are not to be censured for this mode of denominating as long as they recognize the inherent limitations affecting the integrity of the arguments or proofs that follow. Hence, the truth-value of a compound or noncategorical proposition will depend on and be conditioned by the truth-values of its constituent parts. But that which *primarily* determines the truth-value of any compound or noncategorical propositional function is its main constant or sentential connective, for we shall see that each constant or functor has its own distinctive definition and its own operational rules.

It is customary to define a logical constant or logical functor whose chief purpose is to signify a logical operation involving one or more propositional variables by the *truth-table method.*[6] Such a propositional statement is known as a "truth functional" expression. The tabular method is regarded as a convenient instrument for defining logical functors and for determining the logical validity of arguments. Consisting in a simply constructed *schema* somewhat mathematical in appearance, it manifests clearly how the truth-values of any proposition are determined ultimately by its sentential connective. We shall now use this tabular method to derive operational definitions of each of the six constants or functors most commonly employed in logical operations involving categorical and noncategorical propositions.

(1) The *contradictory functor* simply indicates that negation is to be applied to a statement or group of statements taken as a whole. The constant symbolizing this function may appear like a rippled minus sign and is called the *tilde*: e.g., "~p" or "~(p · q)". The tilde is substituted by many non-traditional logicians for such everyday expressions as *it is not the case that*, or, *it is false that*, or simply *not* with a verb: e.g., "It is false that (John Kennedy is President of the U.S.A.)"; "It is not the case that (all saints are Negroes)." Using a propositional variable for each proposition in parentheses and the tilde to express the negation, in complete symbolization the statement would read ~*p*.[7] In seeing the truth-table that is drawn up for the logical definition of this constant or functor it will be clear that the *negation of any true statement becomes false, and the negation of any false statement becomes true or has a true truth-value*:

p	:::	~p
T	:	F
F	:	T

(2) The *conjunctive functor* simply indicates the unity that is designated between propositions by such words used in everyday conversation as *and, moreover, but, although*, and so forth. Written simply as a *dot* this binary functor is always flanked by one or more propositional variables: e.g., "p · q", as the com-

pound conjunctive proposition, "All dogs are animals, *and* all angels are spirits," in complete symbolization would read. In viewing the truth-table constructed for the logical definition of this constant or functor it will be evident that the only condition in which a conjunctive statement has a truth-value of *T* is *when all the constituent propositions are true or have a true truth-value*. Otherwise, compound conjunctive propositional statements, taken as a unit, have a truth-value of *F*:

p	q	:::	p · q
T	T	:	T
T	F	:	F
F	T	:	F
F	F	:	F

(3) The *disjunctive functor* is employed by many nontraditional logicians to signify the so-called *weak* or *noninclusive* type of compound disjunctive statement. Derived from the Latin word "vel," it appears like the letter ∨ and is customarily called the *wedge*: e.g., "p ∨ q." Placed between two or more propositional variables or groups of propositions it expresses the relationship of the sentential connective *either or* (e.g., "*Either* (the students will ride downtown), *or* (they will walk)"). In this example, if propositional variables are substituted for the propositions in parentheses and the wedge functor for the sentential connective, the whole statement is correctly symbolized in this manner: $p \lor q$. In setting up the truth-table by which this constant is logically defined, it will be clear that a compound disjunctive statement taken as a unit has a truth-value of *F only when none of the constitutent propositions has a true truth-value*. Otherwise, a disjunctive statement will always have a truth-value of *T* because at least one of the disjuncts is true or possible of realization:

$$p \; q \; ::: \; p \lor q$$

p q	:	p∨q
T T	:	T
T F	:	T
F T	:	T
F F	:	F

(4) The *alternative functor* is employed by many modern or nontraditional logicians to stand for the *strong* or *exclusive* type of disjunction. Based on the exact meaning of the Latin word "aut," it appears as an *inverted wedge* and designates the strict *either-or* relationship between propositions. It represents the dichotomy that either one course of action or its opposite to a greater or lesser degree is to be chosen, *but not both simultaneously* (e.g., "*Either* this semester exam will be passed, *or* our football hero will not graduate"). In complete symbolization, using propositional variables and the inverted wedge functor, this statement would read $p \land q$. From seeing the tabular definition of this constant it will be clear that a noncategorical alternative statement taken as a whole has a truth-value of *T* under those conditions *when only at least one alternate and at most one of its alternates has a truth-value of T*, i.e., the joint or combined truth of its propositions is definitely excluded:

$$p \; q \; ::: \; p \land q$$

p q	:	p∧q
T T	:	F
T F	:	T
F T	:	T
F F	:	F

(5) The *conditional* or *material implicative functor* is aptly called the *horseshoe*. The exact meaning of this logical function is

the subject of not a little controversy even among nontraditional logicians. It is likewise a dyadic constant, since it logically affects both what precedes and what follows it. This horseshoe-shaped functor is employed to symbolize almost any kind of conditionally inferential relationships between two or more propositional variables or groups of propositions. It takes the place of the sentential connective *if then* or its equivalent expressions (e.g., "*If* there are seven sacraments, *then* it is snowing," or "*If* the majority of the voters in the U.S.A. vote sincerely, *then* he will get the office of President"). In complete symbolization these statements would be written in the same way: $p \supset q$. From the tabular definition of this constant, it is evident that, regardless of the content-relevance or nonrelevance of its antecedent and consequent, the compound statement involving a conditional or material implication taken as a whole has a truth-value of *F* only in that instance *when the antecedent has a true truth-value and the consequent has a false truth-value*. Otherwise, such a noncategorical proposition, taken as a logical unit, has a true truth-value:

p q	:::	$p \supset q$
T T	:	T
T F	:	F
F T	:	T
F F	:	T

(6) The *bi-conditional* or *material equivalence functor* is employed by nontraditional logicians to designate the *if and only if* relationship among propositions or groups of propositions. Appearing as three horizontal bars placed parallel to each other "≡", this symbol is likewise a binary functor (e.g., "*If and only if* he remains a Democrat will he receive that important appointment"). In complete symbolization this noncategorical proposi-

tion would be correctly written in this manner: $p \equiv q$. By the common truth-table method it will be manifest that this truth-functional expression is the equivalent of "If he remains a Democrat then he will receive the important appointment, and if he will receive the important appointment he remains a Democrat." From the tabular definition of this constant it is clear that propositions are materially equivalent only in those conditions in which *both the constitutent propositions or groups of propositions have the very same truth-values*, i.e., either *both are true*, or *both are false*:

p q	:::	p $\equiv$ q
T T	:	T
T F	:	F
F T	:	F
F F	:	T

The functional definitions of these six constants may be more understandable through this schema:

p q	::	~q	:::	p $\cdot$ q	:::	p $\vee$ q	:::	p $\wedge$ q	:::	p $\supset$ q	:::	p $\equiv$ q
T T		F		T		T		F		T		T
T F		T		F		T		T		F		F
F T		X		F		T		T		T		F
F F		X		F		F		F		T		T

Before this section is terminated two important factors of modern logic need to be briefly explained: (a) a popular method of punctuation so as to produce well-formed formulas; and (b) a facile method of constructing truth-tables which have many uses besides definition in logic.

(a) Ambiguous statements are found both in natural languages and in mathematical formulas. Confusion of meaning is not infrequently occasioned by the lack of proper "grouping" of words and phrases, or even by a syntactical error. For example, in the Rule of St. Augustine for happy community living a rather humorous misunderstanding could spring from the following improper grouping of words: "Fast from food and drink as much as your health will allow," if one were to pause after the word *food*. In mathematics too, unless there is proper grouping, the statement or formula is ambiguous in its meaning: e.g., $10 - 2 \times 3$ is a statement that can equal either 4 or 24, depending upon what "grouping" of numerals and operations is intended and followed. Such vagueness of meaning is undesirable in both science and in predication.

Hence logic has to come to grips with this problem of punctuation if it is to serve predication. As far as possible logicians strive for statements that are both exact and clear. To produce well-formed formulas, i.e., truly meaningful statements, some logicians employ a system of punctuation that simply consists of parentheses and brackets. The brackets used are of many shapes and sizes. Other logicians use other punctuational methods.[8] Although parentheses and brackets tend to create a nuisance factor in complex arguments, they seem to be the most convenient method of punctuation and have already been adopted in this chapter. No logical system is without a punctuational method. For practical purposes, then, any bracketed or parenthesized statement is to be treated as a logical unit in itself before any other operation is to be performed: e.g., $(p \lor q) \equiv (\sim p \supset q)$; or, $\sim(\sim p \cdot \sim q)$, a truth-functional expression in which the conjunctive operation is carried on first and then what is bracketed or parenthesized is wholly negated.

(b) Constructing truth-tables can consume a lot of time. We would like to propose one of the easiest procedures for constructing truth-tables under ordinary circumstances. Because truth-tables involving more than five propositional variables are awkward and cumbersome operationally, they become impractical as a decisional procedure for testing the validity of arguments; logicians then employ other efficient methods like the *indirect proof* or the *reductio ad absurdum* and others. But the vexing question for the neophyte logician is how does one figure out the number of horizontal columns and the truth-value sequence in a standardized truth-table. As for the best procedure to determine the number of horizontal columns in any truth-table, one should first count the number of propositional variables employed in the argument. This step is necessary because the number of horizontal columns will be commensurate with and be dependent on the number of propositional variables employed with the same signification and supposition in the argument. This determination is symbolized in a mathematical manner as "2^n"; the "nth" power represents the *number* of propositional variables expressed either affirmatively or negatively: e.g.,

2^1 (prop. var.) will have *two* horizontal columns in its truth-table;

2^2 (prop. var.) will have *four* horizontal columns in its truth-table;

2^3 (prop. var.) will have *eight* horizontal columns in its truth-table;

2^4 (prop. var) will have *sixteen* horizontal columns in its truth-table;

2^5 (prop. var.) will have *thirty-two* horizontal columns in truth-table.

As to the sequence of truth-values that should be followed in constructing a truth-table, one of the most accurate yet convenient procedures to adopt is *to halve successively* the truth-values directly under each propositional variable according to the number of horizontal columns. Perhaps an illustration will help in the understanding of this simple but efficient methodology:

	p	q	r	
	T	T	T̲	
	T	T̲	F	
	T	F	T	
	T̲	F	F	
	F	T	T	
	F	T	F	
	F	F	T	
	F	F	F	

III

The truth-table method is helpful, as we have already seen, in establishing valid definitions for constants or functors. The tabular method also enables logicians to *interdefine* the binary constants, an operation that has many benefits for those being introduced to nontraditional logic. Interdefining is a procedure common to deductive systems of nontraditional logic and it consists in an analysis of the mutual relations between the binary constants themselves. In this section, then, such a study will be undertaken in order that the principal aim of this chapter may be more fully realized. The purposes of this study of the inter-relationship that exists among these constants or functors are fourfold: (1) the validity of the earlier definitions of constants is confirmed and double-checked; (2) the mutual derivability that exists between the functors is made more manifest; (3) the possibility of obverting and converting propositions is logically justified as long as the traditional rules of supposition are not compromised; and (4) the first steps toward an evaluation of the excellence, economy, and elegance of any deductive system will have been taken.[9] In valid interdefining there will result an *identical sequence* of truth-values in the truth-tables involved, if the truth functional expressions are to be considered logically equivalent "by definition" (Df). Our treatment will be brief compared with that of other writers, and no attempt will be made to interdefine the less common binary symbol "$\vee$" and the most controversial binary symbol "$\equiv$."[10]

(1) *Disjunction* (p $\vee$ q) is a logical function that may be interdefined in two ways: (a) in terms of *negation and conjunction*, and (b) in terms of *negation and material implication*. (a) Defined in terms of *negation and conjunction*, we shall see that the truth function "p $\vee$ q" is the same by definition as "$\sim(\sim p \cdot \sim q)$." From the previous section we know that as long as at least one of the propositional variables constituting the noncategorical disjunctive proposition has a true truth-value, the whole statement will have a true truth-value. This is tantamount to denying that both (if only two) propositional variables of the disjunctive statement could have a false truth-value: e.g., "It is false that neither *p* is true nor *q* is true." In short, when it is admitted or given that at least one propositional variable has a true truth-value, it follows that both propositional variables (if only two) are logically excluded from having a false truth-value. This fact and the presence of the necessary *sequential identity* of truth-values between the truth-functional expressions are evident in this illustration:

$\sim$p	p	q	$\sim$q	:::	(p $\vee$ q)	=	$\sim(\sim$p $\cdot$ $\sim$q)	*Df.*
F	T	T	F	:	T		T	(f)
F	T	F	T	:	T		T	(f)
T	F	T	F	:	T		T	(f)
T	F	F	T	:	F		F	(t)

Even greater confirmation of this valid process of interdefining can be shown if the original statement is contradicted, i.e., $\sim$(p $\vee$ q). This can be done simply by appealing to De Morgan's logical law or theorem: *the negation of any disjunction is equivalent to the conjunction of its negated parts.* The previously contradicted statement, "$\sim$(p $\vee$ q)," validly becomes by De

Morgan's law "($\sim$p · $\sim$q)." If this formula is then contradicted it validly becomes "$\sim$($\sim$p · $\sim$q)." This formula would validly be changed to "(p $\vee$ q)" by then applying another of De Morgan's logical laws: *the negation of any conjunction is equivalent to the disjunction of its negated parts.* In such logical mutations there are actually two simple steps to be taken: (1) the tilde outside and in front of the parenthesis by a form of double negation changes the propositional variables $\sim$ p and $\sim$ q into p and q respectively; and (2) the dot functor is changed into the wedge functor symbolizing a disjunction. Perhaps this logical maneuver may be better understood from an example in ordinary language: "Either France continues to be a NATO power, or Russia prospers" is the same statement or propositional form as "It is false both that France will discontinue to be a NATO power and that Russia will not prosper."

(b) Defined in terms of *negation and material implication*, we shall see that the truth functional expression "p $\vee$ q" is the same by definition as "$\sim$p $\supset$ q." In everyday language this means that the following two propositions are logically equivalent: "Either the Yankees will win the World Series or I lose my Barracuda" and "If the Yankees do not win the World Series, then I lose my Barracuda." That such propositional forms are similar is shown tabularly by the process of interdefining in this manner:

$$\sim\text{p} \quad \text{p} \quad \text{q} \sim\text{q} \quad ::: \quad (\text{p} \vee \text{q}) \quad = \quad (\sim\text{p} \supset \text{q}) \, Df.$$

$\sim$p	p	q	$\sim$q		(p $\vee$ q)	($\sim$p $\supset$ q)
F	T	T	F	:	T	T
F	T	F	T	:	T	T
T	F	T	F	:	T	T
T	F	F	T	:	F	F

(2) *Conjunction* (p · q) is a logical function that may be interdefined in two ways: (a) in terms of negation and disjunction, and (b) in terms of negation and material implication. (a) Defined in terms of *negation and disjunction*, we shall see that the

truth function "p · q" is the same by definition as "~(~p ∨ ~q)."
From the previous section we know that only in those instances
when all the constitutent parts have a true truth-value will a noncategorical conjunctive proposition have a true truth-value. In
the realm of everyday language this means that the proposition,
"London is a large city and Toledo is a small city," will be as a
logical unit true only if both categorical propositions have a true
truth-value. By the process of interdefining it will be shown that
the logically equivalent statement of "London is a large city
and Toledo is a small city" is "It is false that either London is
not a large city or that Toledo is not a small city." Since there is
a *sequential identity* in the truth-tables of these truth functional
expressions they are said to be logically equivalent by definition:

$$\sim p \quad p \quad q \sim q \quad ::: \quad (p \cdot q) \quad = \quad \sim(\sim p \vee \sim q) \ Df.$$

~p	p	q	~q	:	(p · q)	~(~p ∨ ~q)	
F	T	T	F	:	T	T	(f)
F	T	F	T	:	F	F	(t)
T	F	T	F	:	F	F	(t)
T	F	F	T	:	F	F	(t)

That this method of interdefining is a valid logical procedure
is clear if the original statement is contradicted, i.e., "~(p · q)"
and then by appealing to De Morgan's law for the negation of a
conjunction the contradicted formula would then be "~p ∨ ~q."
Then by contradicting this already contradicted statement,
"~(~p ∨ ~q)" results. Then by the application of De Morgan's
law for the negation of a disjunction to the last statement we
have the original truth functional expression "p · q". In short,
this interdefinition was derived in two steps: (1) the tilde outside
and in front of the parenthesis by a form of double negation
changes the propositional variables ~*p* and ~*q* into *p* and *q*
respectively; and (2) the wedge functor is changed into the dot
functor symbolizing conjunction.

(b) Defined in terms of *negation and material implication,* we shall see that the truth functional expression "p · q" is the same by definition as "∼(p ⊃ ∼q)." In everyday language this means that the following two noncategorical statements are logically equivalent: "Barry Goldwater will run for the office and he will be defeated" and "It is false that if Barry Goldwater runs for the office then he will not be defeated." The *sequential identity* of these two truth functional statements is obvious from their truth-tables below:

∼p	p	q	∼q	:::	(p · q)	=	∼(p ⊃ ∼q) *Df.*
F	T	T	F	:	T	T	(f)
F	T	F	T	:	F	F	(t)
T	F	T	F	:	F	F	(t)
T	F	F	T	:	F	F	(t)

(3) *Material implication* (p ⊃ q) is a logical function whose exact significance is very much controverted by nontraditional logicians, yet they agree that it can be validly interdefined in two ways: (a) in terms of *negation and disjunction,* and (b) in terms of *negation and conjunction.* (a) Defined in terms of *negation and disjunction,* we shall see that the truth functional expression "p ⊃ q" is the same by definition as "∼p ∨ q". From the previous section we know that only when the antecedent of a conditional statement has a true truth-value and its consequent has a false truth-value is the whole statement said to have a false truth-value. In the concrete, then, the following noncategorical statements are logically equivalent: "If your daughter continues to improve in figure skating, then she will make the Olympic squad" and "Either your daughter discontinues to improve in figure skating, or she will make the Olympic squad." The *sequential identity* of truth values of their respective truth-tables below confirm the logical equivalence of both the functors and the statements:

~p   p   q ~q   :::   (p ⊃ q)   =   (~p ∨ q) *Df.*

~p	p	q	~q	:::	(p ⊃ q)	=	(~p ∨ q)
F	T	T	F	:	T		T
F	T	F	T	:	F		F
T	F	T	F	:	T		T
T	F	F	T	:	T		T

(b) Defined in terms of *negation and conjunction,* we shall see that the truth functional expression "p ⊃ q" is the same by definition as "~(p · ~q)". In the concrete this means that the following two noncategorical statements are logically equivalent: "If your daughter continues to improve in figure skating, then she will make the Olympic squad" and "It is not the case both that your daughter continues to improve in figure skating and that she will not make the Olympic squad." The *sequential identity* of truth values of their respective truth-tables below confirm the logical equivalence of both the functors and the statements:

~p   p   q ~q   :::   (p ⊃ q)   =   ~(p · ~q) *Df.*

~p	p	q	~q	:::	(p ⊃ q)	=	~(p · ~q)	
F	T	T	F	:	T		T	(f)
F	T	F	T	:	F		F	(t)
T	F	T	F	:	T		T	(f)
T	F	F	T	:	T		T	(f)

IV

As we have already seen the truth-tables are not only useful to define the constants or functors that appear in noncategorical statements, but also enable us to interdefine many of these symbols of logical operations. Besides, the truth tabular method is an instrument often used by nontraditional logicians for making definitive decisions on the logical value of moderately complex arguments. The tabular method is of very practical use for arguments up to *five* propositional variables. These are lineally arranged in such a way that their logical value can be easily and effectively determined. By this method or kind of "decisional procedure" complex arguments can be classified with certainty into two general types: (1) *tautologous*, i.e., logically true or valid: (2) *nontautologous*, i.e., logically false or invalid.

An argument or proof is said to be *tautologous*, i.e., logically valid if and only if all the truth-values in the *main column* of its truth-table appear as *T* or *true*. The main column of a truth-table is normally recognized to be that column immediately under the constant or functor with the widest scope or influence. An argument or proof that results in being *tautologous* is in some way, formally or reflectively, a "logical law." The "law of contraposition"—the antecedent and the consequent of any implication or conditional can be validly interchanged provided both these parts are negated—aptly illustrates this logical phenomenon about the main column in a valid argument in the following truth-table:

~p	p	q	~q	:::	$(p \supset q)$	$\equiv$	$(\sim q \supset \sim p)$
						*	
F	T	T	F	:	T	T	T
F	T	F	T	:	F	T	F
T	F	T	F	:	T	T	T
T	F	F	T	:	T	T	T

* indicates the main column.

On the other hand, all arguments that do not satisfy the rigorous demands of logical validity are said to be *nontautologous*, i.e., logically invalid. These invalid arguments or proofs are subdivided into (1) those that are *contingent*, and (2) those that are *contradictory*. An argument-form is considered to be *contingent*, if not all, but at least one of the truth-values in the main column of its truth-table is *false*. Whereas, if all the truth-values in the main column of a truth-table are *false*, then that argument is said to be *contradictory* or totally invalid. Perhaps these notions of invalidity will be more understandable from the following truth-tables:

(1) *Contingent argument*: (i.e., not unconditionally invalid)

~p	p	q	~q	:::	(p ⊃ q)	∨	(~p)
						*	

~p	p	q	~q	:	(p ⊃ q)	∨	(~p)
F	T	T	F	:	T	T	F
F	T	F	T	:	F	F	F
T	F	T	F	:	T	T	T
T	F	F	T	:	T	T	T

* indicates the main column.

(2) *Contradictory argument*: (i.e., under no conditions valid)

~p	p	q	~q	:::	(p ∨ ~p)	⊃	~(q	∨	~q)
						*			

~p	p	q	~q	:	(p ∨ ~p)	⊃	~(q	∨	~q)
F	T	T	F	:	T	F	F	(t)	
F	T	F	T	:	T	F	F	(t)	
T	F	T	F	:	T	F	F	(t)	
T	F	F	T	:	T	F	F	(t)	

* indicates the main column.

In order to make this truth-table method of appraising arguments more relevant we shall take some arguments as they appear in everyday language, translate them into our symbolic notation, and then test their logical value. We shall confine our examples to arguments that need only two or three propositional variables:

(a) *Two propositional variables:* (i.e., $2^n = 2^2$ or *four* horizontal columns)

(1) "If I fall asleep, then I will miss the train. But I did fall asleep. As a result I did miss the train." Substituting the propositional variables "p" for the statement "I fall asleep," and "q" for the statement "I will miss the train," this argument would be written symbolically as indicated in the following truth-table:

~p	p	q	~q	:::	[(p ⊃ q)	·	(p)]	⊃ *	[q]
F	T	T	F	:	(t)	T	(t)	T	T
F	T	F	T	:	(f)	F	(t)	T	F
T	F	T	F	:	(t)	F	(f)	T	T
T	F	F	T	:	(t)	F	(f)	T	F

* indicates the main column.

Comment: With all *T*'s appearing in the main column this argument is evidently *tautologous*. As a matter of fact this argument form is nothing other than the logical law known as the *modus ponens* or as the "law of detachment."[11]

(2) "If I do not fall asleep, then I will not miss the train. Moreover, I will not miss the train. Therefore, I will not fall asleep." Substituting the propositional variables as done above, this argument would be written symbolically as indicated in the following truth-table:

~p	p	q	~q	:::	[(~p ⊃ ~q)	·	(~q)]	⊃ *	[~p]
F	T	T	F	:	(t)	F	(f)	T	F
F	T	F	T	:	(t)	T	(t)	F	F
T	F	T	F	:	(f)	F	(f)	T	T
T	F	F	T	:	(t)	T	(t)	T	T

* indicates the main column.

Comment: With one *F* appearing in the main column this argument is evidently *nontautologous*. The logical law known as the *modus tollens* is violated, and the *fallacy of affirming the consequent* is present.

(b) *Three propositional variables*: (i.e., $2^n = 2^3$ or *eight* horizontal columns)

"If all men have immortal souls, then all men have special inalienable rights. Besides, if all men have such rights, then all men are essentially equal. Therefore, since all men have immortal souls, all men are essentially equal." Substituting the propositional variables "p" for the proposition "All men have immortal souls," and "q" for the proposition "All men have special inalienable rights," and "r" for the proposition "All men are essentially equal," this argument would be written symbolically and registered on a truth-table as follows:

p q r   :::   [(p ⊃ q) • (q ⊃ r)] ⊃ [p ⊃ r]
                                        *

p q r		(p ⊃ q)		(q ⊃ r)	⊃	[p ⊃ r]
T T T	:	(t)	T	(t)	T	T
T T F	:	(t)	F	(f)	T	F
T F T	:	(f)	F	(t)	T	T
T F F	:	(f)	F	(t)	T	F
F T T	:	(t)	T	(t)	T	T
F T F	:	(t)	F	(f)	T	T
F F T	:	(t)	T	(t)	T	T
F F F	:	(t)	T	(t)	T	T

* indicates the main column.

Comment: With all *T*'s appearing in the main column this argument is clearly *tautologous*. The logical law known as the "law of transitivity of implication" is illustrated in this truth-table, a logical law employed hundreds of times by St. Thomas Aquinas throughout his famous *Summa Theologiae*.

Before bringing this introduction to modern or nontraditional logic to a close a brief examination will be made of another common technique for determining the logical value of arguments. When the truth-table method is deemed impractical because the propositional variables in the argument exceed five, nontraditional logicians are wont to employ a vulcanized version of the *reductio ad absurdum* procedure that dates back to Aristotle. Of most methods acceptable to the devotees of the "new logic" for evaluating arguments and proofs, this technique is highly ranked.[12] The *reductio ad absurdum* technique goes beyond establishing the mere *invalidity* of an argument which is achieved if the same truth-values can be assigned consistently to propositional variables so that the premises of the argument are made *true* and the conclusion made *false*.

But such a consistent assignment of truth-values to propositional variables could not be done in a *valid* argument. Hence to establish the *validity* of an argument, regardless of its complexity, no such a truth-value consistency will occur under those stipulated conditions, i.e., *true* truth-values being assigned to the premises and a *false* truth-value to the conclusion. Perhaps an example will make this procedure clear:

$$\begin{array}{ccccccccc} & \text{T} & & & & \text{T} & & & \text{F} \\ (\text{G} \lor \text{H}) & \supset & (\text{I} \cdot \text{J}) & & (\text{J} \lor \text{L}) & \supset & \text{M} & \therefore & (\sim\text{G} \lor \text{M}) \\ \text{t} & ? & \text{t} \quad \text{t} & & \text{t} & ? & \text{t} & & \text{f} \quad \text{f} \end{array}$$

This example, however, needs some explanation. When one employs this technique it is expedient to start the assignation of truth-values with the propositional variables in the conclusion so that as a whole truth function expression it will have a truth-value of *F*. In our example it would mean that both "—G" and "M" are assigned truth-values of *F*. Then, in the first premise of the argument the antecedent "G ∨ H" will have a *true* truth-value since "—G" in the conclusion of the total argument has already been assigned a *false* truth-value. It follows too that if this first premise taken as a logical unit is to have a truth-value of T, then both the propositional variables of its consequent "I · J" must have *true* truth-values. Since the propositional variable "J" is likewise part of the antecedent of the second premise in the argument, it should, to be consistent, retain its *true* truth-value that had already been assigned to it in the first premise. Thus that antecedent has a *true* truth-value, regardless of what truth-value is assigned to the propositional variable "L." But if the second premise taken as a whole truth function is to be properly assigned a truth-value of T as the procedure calls for, then its consequent "M" must be assigned a *true* truth-value. However, such a necessary assignation would be opposed to logical consistency in truth-values because the conclusion of the entire argument could not be assigned a truth-value of F in the beginning of this procedure unless the propositional variable "M" had a *false* truth-value. Since no such consistencies appear in any possible assignation in this argument, it is said to be logically *valid*.

The use of this logical device for appraising complex arguments is encouraged by nontraditional logicians as a valid short-cut method. As a method it is logically sound for it reflects in many ways the need for a *good consequence* in a logically valid argument, a requirement that affects the logicians of both the traditional and nontraditional schools of logic: "in regulating the goodness of any sort of consequence one most universal principle is offered from which the rest are derived and to which they are reduced, namely, that in a good consequence the antecedent cannot be given as true and the consequent as false; but if the antecedent is true, so too the consequent."[13] Thus ends our short study of the noncategorical syllogistic from the nontraditional approach.

Pertinent Quotations about the nontraditional view of the syllogistic:

(a)

Then, in case of a difference of opinion, no discussion between two philosophers will be any longer necessary, as (it is not) between two calculators. It will rather be enough for them to take pen in hand, set themselves to the abacus and (if it so pleases, at the invitation of a friend) say to one another: Calculemus!

Ordinary languages, though mostly helpful for the inferences of thought, are yet subject to countless ambiguities and cannot do the task of a calculus, which is to expose mistakes in inference owing to the forms and structures of words, as solecisms and barbarisms. This remarkable advantage is afforded up to date only by the symbols (notae) of arithmeticians and algebraists, for whom inference consists only in the use of characters, and a mistake in thought and in the calculus is identical.

> —I. M. Bochenski, *A History of Formal Logic* (Notre Dame, Indiana: University of Notre Dame Press, 1961) (taken from G. Leibniz, "Abhdlg. ohne UBERschr. I, 200"), p. 275.

(b)

Exact logic will be that doctrine of the conditions of establishment of stable belief which rests upon perfectly undoubted observations and upon mathematical, that is, upon *diagrammatical,* or *iconic,* thought. We, who are sectaries of "exact" logic, and of "exact" philosophy, in general, maintain that those who follow such methods will, so far as they follow them, escape all error except such as will be speedily corrected after it is once suspected.

> —I. M. Bochenski, *A History of Formal Logic* (Notre Dame, Indiana: University of Notre Dame Press, 1961) (taken from C. S. Peirce, "The regener. Logic" (CP III) 268), p. 280.

(c)

Inference is conducted in my symbolic system (*Begriffsschrift*) according to a kind of calculation. I do not mean this in the narrow sense, as though an algorithm was in control, the same as or similar to that of ordinary addition and multiplication, but in the sense that the whole is algorithmic, with a complex of rules which so regulate the passage from one proposition or from two such to another, that nothing takes place but what is in accordance with these rules. My aim, therefore, is directed to continuous strictness of proof and utmost logical accuracy, along with perspicuity and brevity.

> —I. M. Bochenski, *A History of Formal Logic* (Notre Dame Indiana: University of Notre Dame Press, 1961) (taken from G. Frege, "Grundgesetzen der Arithmetik," (1893), p. 316), p. 284.

Exercises:

(*A*) Employing the "truth-table" method, apply the principles of "interdefining" to the following "truth-functional" expressions in terms of "negation" and any other functor; then translate each into the natural idiom:

(1) $(p \lor \sim q)$

(2) $(\sim p \supset \sim q)$

(3) $(\sim p \cdot \sim q)$

(4) $(p \supset \sim q)$

(5) $\sim (p \cdot \sim q)$

(6) $(\sim p \land q)$

(*B*) By the "truth-table" technique, logically evaluate the following argument-forms and arguments as TAUTOLOGOUS or NON-TAUTOLOGOUS:

(1) *Argument-forms*:

     (a) $[(p \cdot q) \supset r] \equiv [p \supset (q \supset r)]$

     (b) $(\sim p \lor q) \supset (\sim p \supset \sim q)$

     (c) $(q \supset r) \supset [(p \lor q) \supset (p \lor r)]$

     (d) $[p \lor q \lor r] \supset [(\sim p \supset r) \cdot (\sim q \supset r)]$

(2) Arguments:

(a) Either the Mayor will resign, or his wife will have to return those hotel towels and he will have to reduce the sewer tax. But it is not likely that he will reduce the sewer tax. Therefore, it seems to follow that, if she returns those hotel towels, then he will not resign.

(b) If Sam received the telegram then he took the jet plane and will be here for the conference at noon. But I'm afraid Sam didn't take the jet plane. So, it seems it is not false that Sam did not get the telegram.

(c) It is false that both nuclear energy will not be controlled and that the world will stay at peace. However, public sentiment will not allow nuclear energy to be uncontrolled. So, the world will stay at peace.

(*C*) Using the "reductio ad absurdum" method, appraise these complex arguments:

(1) $\sim(\sim A \cdot P) \sim A \therefore P$

(2) $(M \supset N) \cdot (\sim O \lor P); (N \supset Q) \cdot (P \supset R);$

$(Q \supset S) \cdot (\sim R \lor T); \therefore (M \lor O) \supset (S \lor T).$

II

Logic and
Scientific Knowledge

Books have been written solely on "the scientific method" or scientific methods, on their application in the various fields of science, and on the reasons for the distinction of the sciences. For example, John S. Mills in 1848 wrote a book, *A System of Logic*, in an attempt to perfect and update the writings of Francis Bacon, Rene Descartes, and others.[1] In view of these facts the overall aim of this last chapter needs to be quite modest, yet informative. Since logical processes play an important part in producing *science*, we intend to examine them for the purpose of seeing just how each of them contributes to this end. Such a survey study should be helpful because we know from experience that to attempt simultaneously to acquire knowledge in a science (e.g., sociology, theology, chemistry) and to reflect seriously on the method employed to acquire it is an impossible task. Even Aristotle admitted this.[2]

Hence in this chapter we plan to examine three of the most common logical procedures that are alleged to produce *science*. Although they are sometimes painted as separate and disconnected ways to science, we hope to show that they can work together in achieving science because they are only relatively opposed, as are parents and children in a happy family. Generally, a *science* is looked upon as nothing else than a unified body of knowledge composed of principles, causes, and conclusions that are substantively interrelated. The Stagirite was in general agreement with this view but added other conditions, for he thought that science ought to be "certain" and the culmination of a logical procedure known as "demonstration"; these factors should not be lacking in a genuine science.[3] Regardless of one's views on Aristotle's concept of "scientific knowledge," science is never easily achieved. Since the demonstrative procedure depends a great deal on two other logical processes, and since fallacious reasoning is a trap to be avoided by the honest scientist, the principal aim of the chapter will be realized in the following ways: (1) by examining the salient features of *induction* and *dialectics* to the extent that these logical processes or modes of reasoning help to prepare for demonstrative proof; (2) by analyzing the essential notions found in both types of *demonstration* and its relationship to science; and (3) by exposing some of the more common defects of valid and veracious reasoning that tend to develop sophists rather than scientists.

I

(a)

Induction is a form of reasoning that addresses itself to one of the four important questions of human knowledge: *do these things really exist?*[4] Induction has constant reference to factual experiences, moving from the conscious observation of particular objects to a judgment that generalizes about them. Grounded in sensate experiences like smelling odors and hearing sounds, the inductive process always begins with an individual phenomenon or event that leads to a generalization:[5] e.g., after observing the death of one's grandfather, and father, and brother, one with basis concludes that "All men are mortal." Noticing the individual action or reactions of individual entities is the *a posteriori* motion that triggers induction: e.g., observing the self-movement of cockroaches on a bar that indicates they are not just blobs of paint but living entities. If the statements that are to be employed as premises in scientific proofs are not signifying objective realities as they are, then they are useless.

Aristotle insists that the lack of empirical experience lessens our power of taking a comprehensive view of the facts as they are.[6] Data observed under varied conditions, whether naturally or under controlled conditions, is an indispensable part of the inductive procedure. Still, induction is not the mere recording or collecting of the known facts, for generalizations must be made. These generalizations derived from empirical experiences will constitute the premises of a sound scientific argument and frequently enable us to formulate hypotheses as well as confirm them. In short, induction is a logical procedure that enables us to conclude that what is true of a number of individuals of a class or group is true of the whole class or group, or even that what is true under some conditions will be true in similar circumstances at all times. Besides, induction plays no minor role in making first principles and immediate propositions more evident and intelligible.

However, there is a problem about the validity of the inductive process that is constantly being raised. Its validity is challenged by those who question the procedure of obtaining universal propositions about things that exist only as particulars or as individuals. In the next few paragraphs perhaps some light might be cast on the possible solution to this thorny problem; ultimately it is a problem that belongs more in the sphere of epistemology than in logic.

There are two basic assumptions in induction: (1) that the most fundamental principles of reasoning are valid (noncontradiction, identity, and the excluded middle); (2) that there exists a uniformity or similarity in natural things both as to their being and their actions. The first assumption was explained in a previous chapter. The second assumption merely states that *sampling* of particular entities is a safe method or that representative selectivity is a valid practice in science, i.e., that despite their differences as individual entities, things are alike either generically or specifically, or in both ways. Without some sameness or parallelism between entities, science would be impossible.

The generalizations that result in the inductive process are derived from the enumerations of particulars. Looked at from a syllogistic point of view, these enumerations are a kind of middle-term; but in most instances they do not satisfy the condition of universality that should characterize the middle-term in a valid syllogism. This situation is not to be wondered at, for induction is only a step towards such perfection in argumentation. Enumerations in the inductive process can be *complete* or *incomplete*. A *complete* or *exhaustive* enumeration is one in which all the individual members of a class or group are subjected to examination: "All the American League umpires are gentlemen;" "All the Apostles were Semites." This form of enumeration would give certainty, but it is not characteristic of the inductive process because such an enumeration is practically impossible (or even useless) to achieve with most classes or groups.

On the other hand, an enumeration that is *incomplete but sufficient* is the general situation in the inductive procedure, i.e., one that does not include each and every member of a class or group but that does include in its scope the essential factors that distinguish such a class or group. To attempt to generalize without a good quantitative and qualitative "spread" of the individuals in a class or a group is unscientific; whereas an incomplete but sufficient enumeration will have the desired amount of universality about it that signifies a real movement toward scientific knowledge. Even in the most ideal instances induction, especially in the experimental sciences, does not establish a *necessary* connection between a trait and its object that is a requirement for certitude; induction generally offers only *probability* to a greater or lesser degree. It could hardly be otherwise, for only in demonstration is the *necessary* consequence made between the term extremes of the valid syllogism through the middle-term that is genuinely universal.

Examples and arguments "by analogy" are generally classified as inductions. These are popular ways of arguing today. Sometimes one will argue even from a single "typical" case to a generalization. Regardless of the method used, induction has its limitations in producing science; it is by nature not an end in itself. One argues inductively when one states that a special make of automobile, *V*, is a better purchase than all others because it gives more mileage to the gallon of gas, has the latest devices for comfort and safety, has little or no maintenance problems, and because it costs less. Although an induction may be written in syllogistic form, except that its middle-term is a list of individuals, it is not a genuine syllogism: e.g.,

a, b, c, d, e, f, etc. are X.	The auditory powers of dogs, birds, cats, antelopes, etc. are KEEN.
But Y is a, b, c, d, e, f, etc.	*But*: auditory powers for distance are the auditory powers of dogs, birds, cats, antelopes, etc.
Therefore: Y is X.	*Therefore*: auditory powers for distance are keen.

Dialectics has much in common with induction insofar as both are forms of valid reasoning. But one of the chief reasons for their difference is that dialectics addresses itself to another of the four important questions of human knowledge: *what is the real definition of this class of existents*? Like induction, however, it too is a logical process that serves in the development of knowledge in order for it to be "scientific." In other words, dialectical argumentation is not an *end* in itself, but leads us to demonstration. That is how Aristotle viewed the logical process of dialectics which he treated rather thoroughly in the eight books of the *Topics*.

By its nature the dialectical process of thinking is one that is circuitous, zigzaggy, and discursive; sometimes it is even exasperating, because to argue dialectically is to reason from *probable principles* and generally accepted *opinions* about dialectical problems or theses. These problems come in many shapes and sizes: for example, something on which either people hold no opinion either way; or, something the masses hold an opinion on that is contrary or even contradictory to the scientists and philosophers; or, something that is hotly controverted amongst the intelligentsia themselves; or, something that is so vast or intricate that we find it most difficult to give adequate reasons for our answers (e.g., "Is the universe eternal or not?" or "Is the knowledge of opposites the same or not?").

The constant task of the dialectician is to find the most effective and thoroughly neutral line of inquiry about a nontrivial problem about which there are many disparate opinions. By proceeding from the commonly accepted notions about a subject, e.g., *man* (that he has many substantive likenesses with so many other primates), he strives to discover or establish a genuine definitory statement about him. In framing these questions the dialectician is not unlike the heady boxer who comes into the ring with a strategic plan. Aristotle urges dialecticians to observe the following strategy in their discussions: (1) to select cautiously the ground from which the discussion is to be begun; (2) to arrange designedly the sequence of the questions; and (3) to question in such a way as not to defeat the other party but to collaborate in discovering a mutually acceptable definition of the terms employed in the dialectical proposition under examination. In short, then, dialectics is an art of questioning and analyzing the generally accepted opinions on a topic in order to arrive at definitions that then can be used as premises or principles in a demonstrative argument or proof.

The Stagirite suggested four ways by which these objectives can be effectively accomplished, four means that will supply us with reasonings for dialectical problems:[7]

(1) The first way involves the capacity to secure propositions that are both meaningful and problematic, i.e., those questions

to which people answer "yes" and "no." Only real and responsible opinions that are generally accepted, ones that are in accord with the recognized arts and sciences of the day, are worthwhile considering: e.g., "Are there humans on the other planets or not?"; "Is the continuity principle of evolution absolute or not?"; "Ought one to follow his conscience willy-nilly or not?" "Is the knowledge of vice and virtue (opposites) the same or not."

(2) The second way to argue dialectically requires that one is adept at perceiving the many uses and senses of words, for unless it is clear what is actually being proposed it is not easy to discuss it. Ambiguity is one of the greatest threats to a scientific statement and results frequently from the inexact or vague use of words. Besides the confusion of meaning that comes from not distinguishing between univocal and analogical terms, or from identifying the nominal and real meanings of words, Aristotle suggests that we always try to find out whether the "opposite" of the term or expression (its contrary, contradictory, or privative) has more than one meaning: e.g., the contrary of the word *sharp* in the case of a meat-cleaver is *dull*, but in the case of a musical note it is *flat*; or the way the word *sharp* is employed to designate the *tang* of a cheese and the *edge* of a razor. Hence if the opposites of a word or expression have diverse meanings then we can argue that the word itself or the expression itself likewise has diverse meanings.

(3) The third means to proceed effectively as a dialectician is to keep interest in the dialogue or discussion by staying close to the *likenesses* among the things under investigation. This capacity to penetrate to the similarities between things is the forte of a skilled dialectician for in this way agreement and interest prevail in the argumentation (the opponent is still in the ring). Likenesses can be *numerical* (as when one reality is called by different names), *special* (as three men, or three horses), or *general* (as when the term "animal" is attributed to

men and oxen, and the term "quality" is attributed to vice and virtue).

(4) The fourth way to achieve the objectives of dialectics is to be able to discover the *differences* of things. These insights ought as a rule be made from the actions or reactions of entities that are clearly observable through empirical experience. This is usually the sensitive area of most of the problems about which there are clashes of opinions. Differences are generally either *substantive* (as the ability to engage in propositional speech that is proper to man alone of all primates) or *accidental* (as the state of health or sickness in which one finds himself). As we learned earlier, accidental differences far outnumber substantive ones. Aristotle gives this means a tremendous importance in dialectics because of its intimate relationship with establishing a definition and the important role that a genuine definition can play as a premise in a demonstration.

Dialectics, then, is a most useful logical process in any scientific endeavor involving a problem about which there are many well-founded opinions. Each type of science can tailor the process to suit itself, for it is most helpful in scientific research. As an intellectual training, dialectics prepares one for the casual encounters experienced in everyday living and for any form of academic adventure. With the ability to raise searching questions on both sides of an important problem, with the honesty to argue for both sides of the problem extensively, we will often be forced to settle for the more probable answer in light of the inconclusivenss of the evidence. Dialectics, finally, shows us what still needs to be cleared away before certitude becomes a reality.[8]

II

Unlike induction and dialectics, *demonstration* is a "terminative" type of discourse.[9] Yet, as we have seen already, both these logical processes are indispensable instruments in preparing for a demonstrative argument or proof; they assure us that special classes of entities really exist and have real definitions. Dissatisfied with the notions of science in his day, Aristotle was quite original in the formulation of his theory on demonstration ('ἀποδείξις) which he formally treated as an instrument of science in his logical works *Posterior Analytics I* and *II*.[10] In these books the Stagirite shows us how demonstration is a logical process that principally addresses itself to the two most important questions of human knowledge: (1) *Is the connection of an attribute with an entity an incontrovertible fact?*, and (2) *What is the chief reason for this connection?*

Perhaps a brief explanation of the notions of "scientific knowledge" and "certitude" might be helpful in understanding the role that demonstrative discourse can play in the world of science. To know an entity or a class of entities by its proper causes or principles is what is meant by *certain and scientific knowledge* in the best sense of both terms. Naturally in the movement of "knowing" the human intellect tends to come to a kind of rest upon knowing *what* an entity is (its material and formal causes) and *why* it is as it is and is necessarily incapable of being otherwise than it is. This stamp of certainty is characteristic of a proposition or a group of conclusions worthy to be labeled *scientific* or *sciental*. Such excellence in knowledge is considered to be possible of attainment by Aristotle through the instrumentality of *demonstration* (propter quid) and is also considered to be the prime analogate in all types of sciental knowing.

Both certitude and science, then, admit of degrees of perfection; one science can be more perfect than another science, like one class of animals can be more perfect knowers than other classes. Nevertheless, although it is possible to rank sciences according to various standards (e.g., theoretical and practical), one science is not essentially more a *science* than another. That certitude is likewise an analogical notion in no way diminishes the intrinsic value of what is established discursively and validly in a science. This phenomenon is reasonable enough to understand if you consider the differences in the subject matter of sciences (chemistry, mathematics, optics, metaphysics, and theology) and the peculiar nature of science itself. Located between the boundaries of the immediate knowledge of ideas on the one hand, immediate knowledge of the first principles of thought on the other hand, any *science* is a *mediated* type of knowledge.[11] It is an organized body of knowledge in which its conclusions are validly derived from its own proper principles which, in turn, are derived from a higher science, for no science proves its own principles.

With that orientation on the notions of *science* and *certitude*, the meaning of demonstrative discourse may be clearer by the following examples which are alleged to be demonstrations:

> (a) A fluid of limited quantity kept in perpetual motion in one direction is moved circularly; but the blood is such a fluid; therefore, the blood is moved circularly.[12]

> (b) Every figure made up of three straight lines has an exterior angle equal to two interior mutually opposed angles; but every triangle is such a figure; therefore, every triangle has an exterior angle equal to two interior mutually opposed angles.[13]

> (c) At the core of the universe each soul exists for God; but all reality, especially material reality that surrounds us, exists for our souls; hence, all such reality exists through our souls for God.[14]

> (d) Every habit inclining us to happiness is a habit that is operating in harmony with right reason; but virtue is a habit operating according to right reason; therefore, virtue is a habit inclining us to happiness.[15]

Aristotle offered two *definitions* of demonstration: one from the point of view of its final cause, and the other from the point of view of its material cause.[16] To define demonstration as *a valid syllogistic argument that is productive of sciental knowledge* is to state that on account of which a thing is, its final cause or purpose. In other words, demonstrative discourse aims at making us truly knowledgeable about things as they objectively exist; it is a logical process that generates in us the intellectual habit called *science*. On the part of matter, demonstration must satisfy rigid conditions as to its premises; these *premises must be true, primary, immediate, better known than and prior to and causes of its conclusion.* In short, scientific conclusions must flow from scientific premises in any genuine demonstrative syllogism, for it is valid reasoning to a necessary conclusion.

Only the second definition of demonstration needs some further explanation. There is some overlapping evident in these conditions. Of the six conditions that premises in demonstrative discourse are expected to satisfy, three of them are somewhat absolute and three of them are somewhat relative. The three conditions which are *somewhat absolute* are that the premises should be *true, primary,* and *immediate*:

(a) *True* premises alone can generate a true conclusion. We have already seen why it is invalid reasoning to have a false conclusion derived from true premises. Then, too, nonexistents are incapable of being known (e.g., that the diagonal of a square is identical with its side), still in no way does this condition mean that every truth must be demonstrable. True premises are of two types: (1) those that are already proved; (2) those that are self-evident. Self-evident propositions are those in which the predicate is included in the essence of the subject, as in the proposition "Every virtue is a quality" the word *quality* forms an essential part of virtue. Self-evident propositions are so *to us* if the essence of both the predicate and the subject is known to us; some of these propositions can be absolutely self-evident, i.e., known to all (e.g., a whole is greater than any of its parts); others can be relatively self-evident, i.e., known only to some who may be knowledgeable in a special area like medicine or philosophy or chemistry. However, if the essence of the predicate and the subject of a proposition are not known to us, yet the predicate is contained in the quiddity of the subject, then that proposition is said to be *self-evident in itself but not to us* (e.g., God exists). Hence, such propositions would have to be proved.

(b) *Primary* premises are those propositions or principles from which ultimately all valid syllogisms are derived. They are the

appropriate and basic verities in their own proper order or genus
to which all others are reducible and which by themselves have
an appeal that is convincing.

(c) *Immediate* premises are those that are said to be "per se
known" for they lack the medium necessary for being demonstrated, i.e., they are indemonstrable for there are no propositions
that are prior to them.

On the other hand, the three conditions which premises in
demonstrative discourse are expected to satisfy that are *somewhat
relative*, i.e., in relation to the *necessity of its conclusion*, are that
they should be *better known than* and *prior to* and *causes of its
conclusion*.

(a) Premises are said to be *better known than* the conclusion
because they are antecedently known to it. This antecedent
knowledge, however, is not merely an understanding of the
meaning but knowledge of the fact as well. These premises ought
to be better known too because when they cause a manifestation
of the necessary conclusion through the principles being known,
it follows that they themselves ought to be better known. Still
Aristotle is aware of the ambivalence of this condition insofar
as particular objects or objects of sense can be better known
to man than the most universal causes which are not so close.

(b) Premises are said to be *prior to* the conclusion more in
the order of truth than in the order of time because it is through
knowing the truth of the premises that we know the truth of the
conclusion of the demonstrative argument, for it is natural to
man to proceed from what is more known to what is less known.

(c) Premises are said to be the *causes of the conclusion* because it is brought into existence through them and because we
possess scientific knowledge of an entity only when we know its
causes. In demonstration this causality is brought about chiefly
through the middle-term which unites the premises and hence

produces the necessary conclusion as an effect. Although the middle-term is able to undergo variations, it must be both necessary and distributed; besides being related to the extremes in the demonstrative syllogism, the middle-term must be of the same genus yet prior and better known than the extremes.

Aristotelians are in substantial agreement that demonstrative discourse is adequately divided into two kinds, one more perfect than the other: (1) *demonstration by proper cause or "propter quid"*; and (2) *demonstration of the fact or "quia."* Since the more perfect of the two types is considered to be the demonstration by proper cause or "propter quid" it is said to be the primary analogate. Each of the two types of demonstration need some explanation.

(1) *Demonstration by proper cause or "propter quid"* produces truth through a knowledge of the proximate cause on account of which a thing is of such a type, i.e., it gives that cause which is and said to be convertible per se with its principal effect. In other words, in this type of demonstration there is shown the radical cause that is necessarily responsible for the identification of the predicate with the subject in this necessary conclusion. This kind of demonstrative discourse is obtained ordinarily when the middle-term is the real definition of the subject through which we show that a genuine property belongs to the subject of the necessary conclusion, as shown in the previous examples.

(2) *Demonstration of the fact or "quia,"* on the other hand, is the kind that only intends to show clearly and evidently that something is true, i.e., that it is truly given, but not by considering how it is true or why it is true. In other words, demonstration "quia" is the one that is concerned about some truth not so much in exposing it through its proper and peculiar root or cause, but rather in showing it either through its remote cause (that which is not convertible with its effect) or its effect or something else with which that truth has an essential connection although it does not result from it. In short, this type of demonstrative discourse

proves the truth of a conclusion but without uncovering the proximate cause of the truth, for it proceeds usually from an effect or remote cause in the premises to the cause in the conclusion. For example, when one argues from the existence of a jetplane as an effect to the existence of engineers as its cause in the conclusion, one is arguing in this type of demonstrative mode; likewise when one employs the term *animal* as a remote cause of man's unique ability to be a toolmaker, for *animal* is a generic notion only in relation to any predication about man. It is evident that *animal* and *toolmaker* are not convertible terms. In the examples given earlier there are at least two instances of a demonstration of the fact or "quia"; the classical example of this type of demonstration is found in the *Summa Theologiae* (Part I, Quest. 2, Art. 3) of Saint Thomas Aquinas on "whether God exists."

III

Since the final cause of logic is to help those who are interested in the personal acquisition and possession of sciental knowledge, scientists ought to be acquainted with the ways that lead to *defective* argumentation. Erroneous manners of reasoning are multiple, as we have already seen. Still it is a fact that most mistakes in reasoning are not commited *intentionally*; we fall unwittingly into most of our errors in dialogue or discussions. However, in every period of history there have been people who intentionally discourse in a manner that only masquerades as *scientific*. Such people are called *sophists*, for they prefer to appear to be wise rather than to be wise. A sophist is one who uses the techniques of the dialectician but only with a pretense to be scientific. In short, fallacious reasoning is the deliberate design of the sophist for he is a counterfeit scientist. In order to avoid fallacies in argumentation, and in order to be able to detect them in others who employ them against us, these are our principal reasons for making this study of fallacious reasoning.

Throughout this book we have come across various types of fallacies, for they always spring up from some violation of reasoning that is related to a lack of perfection either in syntax, in diction, or in knowledge itself. In his *De Sophisticis Elenchis*, Aristotle gave a rather detailed treatment (34 chapters) to fallacies and showed how they would best be refuted. He enumerates thirteen different types of fallacious reasoning, but also observes that there are ultimately only two fonts from which they flow: (1) *from language*; or (2) *from something other than language*. The Stagirite points out that not a few of these errors are easy to detect, while others are very difficult to detect and can elude even the most expert logicians. To examine at any length all thirteen fallacies is not necessary to achieve the principal end of this section, and it would be needlessly repetitious of many of the logical notions that have already been adequately considered in preceding chapters. Hence, our treatment will be both economical and relevant.

(1) *From language*, according to Aristotle, *six* fallacies in argumentation can arise and they are known as: *equivocation, amphiboly, accent, form of expression,* and *combination-division.* Actually, from the point of view of logic, these are reducible to errors either in *signification* (e.g., equivocation) or in *supposition* (e.g., form of expression). Amphiboly is a mistake more in syntax than in logic (e.g., dangling modifiers); accent is chiefly an error in diction. The fallacies of composition and division occur mostly because of an unwarranted use of supposition in a conclusion or in the premises of an argument, for they consist in joining or separating notions in the conclusion that were not so united or divided in the premises: e.g., Every man is capable of spontaneous conversation; but every man is also vegetative; hence every vegetative being is capable of spontaneous conversation.

(2) *From something other than language*, according to Aristotle, *seven* fallacies in argumentation can arise and they are known as: *accident, relative to the absolute, affirming the consequent, the false cause, begging the question, the complex question,* and *ignoring the issue.* Actually, from the point of view of logic,

these are reducible to *errors in sciental knowing* (e.g., confusing
an accidental attribute of a thing with what is essential to it, and
supposing that something is the cause of an effect when objectively it is not so) or *errors in valid syllogizing* (e.g., affirming the
consequent). The other four fallacies are likewise violations of
the rules governing valid syllogizing. Since premises in scientific
argumentation are the *causes* of a conclusion, premises that are
not related causally to the conclusion are responsible for both
ignoring the issue and begging the question or what is sometimes
called "arguing in a circle." The fallacy of the complex question
is nothing else than the so-called "loaded question": e.g., "Is your
wife still drinking?"; the implications of the question are hardly
answerable by a simple "yes" or "no." The fallacy of arguing
from the relative to the absolute is a violation of the rule about
overdistributing an extreme in the conclusion or else is a case
of an undistributed middle-term; this fallacy occurs frequently
and consists in judging all members of a religious class or an
ethnic group "guilty" because of the conduct of a few in that
class or group.

Finally, it should be observed that the fallacy of ignoring the
issue comes in many packages: e.g., attacking the opponent and
not the problem, or threatening one's opponent with harm to himself or loved ones, or by a rhetorical appeal to the mob, or by a
clever appeal to one expertise in one field of learning other than
the one in which the dispute is located. The argument *ad homi-
nem* is one in which the issue is obfuscated or ignored by an attack on the moral integrity or the academic abilities of one's opponent: e.g., how can one know what purity is if one does not
practice it. The argument *ad baculum* (stick or club) is one in
which personal harm is threatened to the extent that the argument is ended or conceded because of fear, not truth. The argument *ad populum* is one employed mostly by dictators and
politicians, for it is nothing else than an emotional appeal to the
prejudices of the masses: e.g., Castro's trials. The argument *ad
verecundiam* is the most subtle and the most deadly because it is
usually so sophisticated. Its aim is to *shame* one's opponent or
opponents into agreement with a thesis by arguing from the repu-

tation of excellence a savant has in one field, say mathematics or music, to his views in quite another field of learning, say ethics or theology: e.g., an anthropologist seeking to deny freedom of the will in humans by appealing to the statements of some well-known chemical engineer.

Footnotes

INTRODUCTION:

1 See *The Basic Works of Aristotle*, tr. Richard McKeon (New York: Random House, 1941), "On the Parts of Animals," I, 1, p. 643. N.B. This edition is signified unless otherwise indicated.

2 See Mortimer Adler, *The Difference of Man and the Difference It Makes* (New York: Holt, Rinehart and Winston, 1967), especially chapter 12.

3 See Robert W. Schmidt, S.J., *The Domain of Logic according to Saint Thomas Aquinas* (The Hague: Martinus Nijhoff, 1966), pp. 75–165.

4 See Saint Thomas Aquinas, *Commentary on Aristotle's Posterior Analytics I*, lesson 1 (Leonine edition of the *Opera Omnia*).

5 Thomas Gilby, O.P., *Barbara Celarent* (London: Longmans Green and Co., 1949), p. 3n.

6 See Bertrand Russell, *Unpopular Essays* (New York: Simon and Schuster, 1951), pp. 35–50.

7 Cf. Alfred Tarski, *Logic, Semantics, and Mathematics* (New York: Oxford Press, 1956); and Alfred Ayer, *Language, Truth and Logic* (New York: Dover Publ., 2nd rev. ed., 1952), pp. 45–75.

8 See I. Copi, *Symbolic Logic* (New York: MacMillan Co., 1954), p. 21; and Saint Thomas Aquinas, *ibid.*, "De Potentia," VI, 1, ad 11: "the logician and mathematician consider things only according to their formal principles" (author's transl.).

CHAPTER 1, "*Words and Predication*":

1 See Louis Lachance, O.P., "The Philosophy of Language," *The Thomist*, IV (1942), pp. 547–588; some Ontologists claim that God

is proximately responsible for the origin and evolution of language; many French sociologists say the impact of society itself is the cause; other thinkers espouse some brand of Nominalism, claiming that the word-symbol itself and a thing's essence are the identically same entity.

2 See Saint Thomas Aquinas, *Summa Theologiae*, Part I, Q. 106.

3 See M. Adler, *ibid*, chs. 10–12.

4 See L. M. Regis, O.P., *Epistemology*, tr. Imelda C. Byrne (New York: The MacMillan Co., 1959), especially Parts II and III.

5 See I. M. Bochenski, O.P., *A History of Formal Logic*, tr. Ivo Thomas, O.P. (Notre Dame, Indiana: Univ. of Notre Dame Press, 1961), pp. 25–145.

6 Cf. the position of Lachance noted above with H. H. Price, *Thinking and Experience* (London: Hutchinson's University Library, 1953); also C. J. Herrick, *The Evolution of Human Nature* (Austin, Texas: Univ. of Texas Press, 1956); New York, Harper Torchbooks, 1961.

CHAPTER 2, *"Concepts and Predication"*:

1 Aristotle, "Metaphysics IV," ch. 7.

2 See Aristotle, "Topics I," ch. 5; also Saint Thomas Aquinas, *Commentary on Aristotle's Posterior Analytics I*, 13, n. 2.

3 See *ibid.*; also *Summa Theol.* I, q. 77, a. 1, ad 5; and the *Contra Gentes II*, 91.

4 See H. H. Price, *Thinking and Experience* (London: Hutchinson's Library, 1953); and Karl Popper, *Conjectures and Refutations* (New York: Basic Books, 1962), especially pp. 290–98.

5 See Peter of Spain (Pope John XXI), *Summulae Logicales*, tract 2, 2, 13 (Marietti edit.: p. 19, author's translation).

6 See Vincent E. Smith, *Footnotes for the Atom* (Milwaukee: Bruce Publ., 1951), ch. 2 and ch. 4; and Anthony Standen, *Science Is a Sacred Cow* (New York: E. P. Dutton Co., 1950), chs. 1, 3, and 5.

7 See Aristotle, "Metaphysics XII," ch. 5.

8 See Aristotle, "Categories," chs. 6–10.

9 These matters have been analyzed sufficiently by I. Bochenski in his classical work, *A History of Formal Logic*, previously mentioned, pp. 272–273.

CHAPTER 3, *"Definition and Predication"*:

1 Aristotle treats the problem of definition in many places in the *Topics I*, *Posterior Analytics II*, and *Metaphysics VII, VIII*. Much of our material will be based on his dialectical treatment in these places.

2 Aristotle, "Posterior Analytics II," ch. 3.

3 See Aristotle, "Nichomachean Ethics I," ch. 3; also V. E. Smith, *Philosophical Physics* (New York: Harper Bros., 1950); and W. H. Kane, "The First Principles of Changeable Being," *The Thomist*, VIII (1945), pp. 35–45.

4 Aristotle, "Metaphysics VII," ch. 4.

5 See *Systema Natura* by Carl Von Linne (1707–1778), the Swedish botanist who employed this methodology and terminology in his scientific classifications which are still current.

6 See his *Commentary on Aristotle's Posterior Analytics II*, less. 16.

7 See Aristotle, "Posterior Analytics II," ch. 5, and "Prior Analytics I," ch. 31.

8 For functional purposes in this book the term *connotation* can be identified more or less with the intension or comprehension of a concept (idea), i.e., the perfections in an essence.

9 This fact is especially evident in the works cited in footnote 1.

10 See Aristotle, "Metaphysics VII," ch. 12, and "Topics I," ch. 5.

11 See A. H. Bassoon and D. J. O'Connor, *Introduction to Symbolic Logic* (Illinois: The Free Press, 1960), esp. pp. 27–29.

12 See Aristotle, "Categories," ch. 1.

CHAPTER 4, *"Propositions and Predication"*:

1 See I. M. Bochenski, O.P., *A History of Formal Logic*, tr. Ivo Thomas, O.P. (Notre Dame, Indiana: Univ. of Notre Dame Press, 1961), p. 162.

2 Sometimes this part of the *Organon* is called the *Peri Hermeneas* or the *Hermeneia*. It and *Posterior Analytics II* came early in the development of Aristotle's system of logic, according to Bochenski (*ibid.*, pp. 42–44).

CHAPTER 5, *"Kinds of Propositions"*:

1 See P. Suppes, *Introduction to Logic* (Princeton, New Jersey: D. Van Nostrand Co., 1957), p. 12.

2 See Saint Thomas Aquinas, "About the Enunciation" (Opusculum 48).

3 N.B.: Most often, any being that is uniquely singular may be considered UNIVERSAL in determining the quantity of the proposition (e.g., God).

4 See I. Copi, *Introduction to Logic* (New York: The MacMillan Co., 1953), pp. 290–298.

5 See Aristotle, "On Interpretation," ch. 5.

6 See the text from Peter of Spain printed at the end of this chapter.

7 See Bochenski, *op. cit.*, pp. 119–120.

8 See Jan Lukasiewicz, "On a Controversial Problem of Aristotle's Modal Syllogistic," in *Dominican Studies*, VII (1954), pp. 114–128.

9 See Aristotle, "Metaphysics V," ch. 5.

CHAPTER 6, *"Properties of the Categorical Proposition"*:

1 The *enthymeme* is sometimes called the "truncated syllogism," and will be analyzed in a later chapter. It is a shortened form of syllogistic reasoning in which one premise is purposely omitted or suppressed. It is employed often in advertising, in public speeches, and in ordinary social intercourse.

2 See I. Copi, *Introduction to Logic* (New York: The MacMillan Co., 1953), pp. 154–160. Since *second intentions* are the principal concern of the logician, he should have only a minimal interest in the existential element of entities. Perhaps that is why Aristotle, the Peripatetic, employs term variables (x, y, z) in explaining some of his theories about logical entities and processes.

3 See John of St. Thomas, *Cursus Philosophicus Thomisticus*, Book I, "Logica," I, 2, chs. 9–15 for an extensive analysis of other properties (ampliation, restriction, appellation, etc.); see also Peter of Spain, *Summulae Logicales*, VII, 9–11.

4 Aristotle, "On Interpretation," ch. 6.

5 Saint Thomas Aquinas, *Commentary on Aristotle's On Interpretation*, lesson 9 (author's transl.)

6 The Square of Opposition is a visual aid devised in antiquity. Aristotle and other ancient Hellenic philosophers often made use of such aids to help their students (e.g., see ch. 10 of *On Interpretation*). In modern times, Venn's diagrams and Euler's circles were more sophisticated constructs for explaining the same logical entities. Categorical propositions have been represented in circular, angular, and elliptical figures. Here are examples of some of Venn's compartmental forms:

(a) No men are angels:

(b) All men are animals:

(c) Some Americans are Communists:

(d) Some Africans are not Communists:

7 As indicated earlier, an *A* proposition that signifies as a perfect definition (e.g., Every man is risible; All virtues are good habits) is convertible simply only because of its peculiar subject-matter. In other words, the *universal affirmative, A*, in its formal structure validly converts accidentally; however, because of this accidental or material consideration, it does on such occasions have this capacity for a simple interchange of its extremes.

CHAPTER 7, *"Argumentation"*:

1 See *Summa Theologiae* I, q. 85, art. 5, or text "(b)" at the end of the chapter.

2 See John of St. Thomas, *Cursus Philosophicus Thomisticus*, "Logica," part I, illustr. 8, art. I, or text "(c)" at the end of the chapter.

3 See text "(g)" at the end of the chapter.

4 Aristotle, "Prior Analytics I," ch. 4.

5 I. M. Bochenski, O.P., *A History of Formal Logic*, tr. Ivo Thomas, O.P. (Notre Dame, Indiana: Notre Dame Univ. Press, 1961), p. 70. These discoveries were: use of term-variables, formal treatment, and axiomatization.

6 Sir W. D. Ross, *Aristotle's Prior and Posterior Analytics*, rev. ed. (Oxford: Clarendon Press, 1957), esp. pp. 24, 29.

7 See Jan Lukasiewicz, *Aristotle's Syllogistic*, 2d ed. (Oxford: Clarendon Press, 1957), p. 7: "The introduction of variables into logic is one of Aristotle's greatest inventions. It is almost incredible that till now, as far as I know, no one philosopher or philologist has drawn attention to this most important fact. I venture to say that they must all have been bad mathematicians, for every mathematician knows that the introduction of variables into arithmetic began a new epoch in that science."

8 As evidence for this view, see especially Plato's *The Republic, The Sophist*, and *The Phaedo*. In his scholarly study of this matter, Fr. Joseph T. Clark, S.J., points out that Aristotle also depended upon the unique contributions of Eudoxus (400–347 B.C.), who had worked out the techniques of proportion; see his *Conventional Logic and Modern Logic* (Woodstock, Maryland: Woodstock Press, 1952), pp. 5–8.

9 Among those who have given critical attention to Aristotle's theory of the syllogism are Sextus Empiricus, the Stoics, Alexander of Aphrodisias, Theophrastus, Peter Ramus, I. Kant, A. de Morgan, Albert the Great, Thomas Aquinas, J. Lukasiewicz, Ivo Thomas, Charles S. Peirce, A. N. Prior, J. Veatch, and H. Joseph; also see M. R. Cohen and E. Nagle, *An Introduction to Logic and Scientific*

Method (London: Routledge and Kegan Paul Ltd., 1934), in the 1963 paperback ed. pp. 176–181 for a brief but lucid discussion of the syllogism and its *petitio principii* problem.

10 See Aristotle, "Posterior Analytics II," ch. 16.
11 A. N. Prior, *Formal Logic* (Oxford: Clarendon Press, 1955), p. 116.
12 See Aristotle, "Prior Analytics I," ch. 4.
13 Bochenski, p. 69.
14 See Bochenski, pp. 140–142; and Lukasiewicz, pp. 38–42.

CHAPTER 8, *"Validity of Categorical Syllogisms"*:

1 See Aristotle, "On the Parts of Animals I," ch. 1.
2 Aristotle, "Prior Analytics I," ch. 4; also see ch. 24, 85b 23–28, for the notion of *demonstration* insofar as it is a syllogism that produces scientific knowledge. Demonstration will be treated in our chapter XI.
3 See Aristotle, "Metaphysics IV," ch. 3.
4 See Aristotle, "Metaphysics XI," ch. 5.
5 See Aristotle, "Prior Analytics I," ch. 46, also ch. 32; and "Metaphysics IV," chs. 3 and 7 in which there is a laudable defense of the validity of the *excluded middle* principle.
6 Cf. such scholars' views as Ockham (Occam), W. D. Ross, John of St. Thomas, A. N. Prior, J. N. Keynes in his *Formal Logic*, p. 301, and Fr. I. Bochenski, O.P., in *A History of Formal Logic*, p. 79. Jan Lukasiewicz seems to hold quite opposite opinions in his *Aristotle's Syllogistic*, pp. 43–47, insofar as he favors Barbara and Celarent as the two perfect moods in the first figure as the most economical set of axioms. Still others such as Bochenski think that the "dictum de omni et nullo" is fully applicable only to the first figure. Finally, we can note for the sake of completeness that some logicians tend to employ "dicta" that have some affinity to those already mentioned; as parts of the theory on the categorical syllogism, they would like to include the "dictum de diverso" and the "dictum de exemplo" and the "dictum de parte," as can be seen in A. N. Prior, *Formal Logic*, p. 112.
7 The next footnotes locate mostly in the "Analytics" each of these proximate logical rules or norms; they are stated there either explicitly or implicitly.
8 See Aristotle, "Prior Analytics I," ch. 25, also ch. 5.
9 Aristotle, "Prior Analytics II," ch. 19.
10 See Aristotle, "Metaphysics I," ch. 2.
11 Aristotle, "Prior Analytics I," ch. 4.
12 *Ibid.*, ch. 24 and ch. 6.
13 *Ibid.*, ch. 6.
14 *Ibid.*, ch. 4.

15 *Ibid.*, ch. 5, 27a.
16 *Ibid.*, ch. 24, 41b.
17 See *ibid.*, ch. 7; also "Posterior Analytics I," ch. 14.
18 Aristotle, "Prior Analytics I," ch. 1, 24b; also ch. 5, 28a; and ch. 6, 29a.
19 Aristotle, "Posterior Analytics I," ch. 14, 79a.
20 See Aristotle, "Prior Analytics II," ch. 9.
21 See Aristotle, "Rhetoric I," chs. 20–25, and "Rhetoric II," chs. 23–25; also his "On Sophistical Refutations."
22 See Saint Thomas Aquinas, *Commentary on the Posterior Analytics I*, ch. 1, less. 1, 12, where he explicitly refers to the enthymeme as a "truncated" (detruncatus) syllogism.
23 See W. V. Quine, *Methods of Logic* (New York: Henry Holt Co., 1950), pp. 185–189, for some good insights on the enthymeme.
24 See Aristotle, "Prior Analytics I," ch. 25.
25 See G. Leibniz, *Confession of Nature against Atheists* (1668).

CHAPTER 9, *"The Noncategorical Syllogistic (traditional presentation)"*:

1 See our article, "Ecumenism in Logic," *The Thomist*, Vol. 31 (July, 1967).
2 See W. V. Quine, *Methods of Logic* (New York: Henry Holt Co., 1950), pp. 12–17.
3 See Peter of Spain's text at end of chapter.
4 *The Works of Aristotle Translated into English*, Vol. I, transl. and edit. W. D. Ross (Oxford: University Press, 1928), "Prior Analytics II," ch. 4, 57b; also see his "De Soph. Elench." ch. 5 in the same volume.
5 See Bochenski, *op. cit.*, pp. 11–13.
6 See W. V. Quine, *ibid.*, pp. 11–13.

CHAPTER 10, *"Noncategorical Syllogistic (nontraditional presentation)"*:

1 See W. M. Kneale, *The Development of Logic* (Oxford: University Press, 1962), pp. 378–383.
2 The names of these works are: *Mathematical Analysis of Logic* (1847) and *The Investigation of the Laws of Thought* (1854).
3 This listing is meant to be neither a complete nor an exhaustive enumeration. Rather it is intended merely to show that much scholarship has been going on rather quietly, but inexorably, for well over a century in this field. Yet it is both anomalous and lamentable that so few logicians of the traditional school, until rather recently, have been taking this development seriously.

4 These radical differences in symbolizing are obvious in the stroke function of Sheffer "/" and also in the notations of Lukasiewicz: e.g., "Cppp."

5 These symbols of truth functions can be easily found in the writings of G. Peano (1858–1932), especially in the second tome of his monumental work entitled "Formulaire de Mathematiques" (1895–1908), and also in the famous "Principia Mathematica" (1910) of Bertrand Russell and A. N. Whitehead.

6 It is an historical fact that the ancient Megarians employed this methodology and that it was perfected by Frege, Peirce, and Wittgenstein.

7 Sometimes logicians prefer to superimpose the negation or contradictory symbol on the propositional variable itself: e.g., $"\overline{p}"$; either notational system is acceptable.

8 Some logical systems use a punctuational system comprised of dots: e.g., $"\:"\;"\:.,"$ etc. in lieu of parentheses and brackets; other logical systems, as in that of Lukasiewicz, have an economically built-in notation in their functional statements that is so tailored as to make any form of bracketing unnecessary: e.g., Cppp (*If* p and p *then* p).

9 See A. N. Prior, *Formal Logic* (Oxford : Clarendon Press, 1955), pp. 230–235.

10 See W. V. Quine, *Methods of Logic* (New York: Henry Holt & Co., 1955), pp. 35–55.

11 See Patrick Suppes, *Introduction to Logic* (New York: D. Van Nostrand Co. Inc., 1959), pp. 32–34.

12 See I. Copi, *Symbolic Logic* (New York: The MacMillan Co., 1954), pp. 63–65.

13 John of St. Thomas, *Cursus Philosophicus Thomisticus*, "Logica," Tome I, bk. 3, ch. 11 (author's transl.).

CHAPTER 11, *"Logic and Scientific Knowledge"*:

1 Cf. J. S. Mills (1806–1873), *A System of Logic*, for his views on induction and his famous canons of experimental inquiry; and the critical analysis recently done by I. Copi, *Introduction to Logic* (New York: The MacMillan Co., 1955), especially pp. 363–377; and Francis Bacon (1561–1626) in his *Novum Organon* and Rene Descartes (1596–1650) in his *Discourse on Method*.

2 See Aristotle, "Metaphysics II," ch. 3.

3 See Aristotle, "Posterior Analytics I," ch. 2.

4 See Aristotle, "Posterior Analytics II," ch. 1.

5 See Saint Thomas Aquinas, *Commentary on Posterior Analytics I*, lect.1.

6 As an example, see Aristotle, "On Generation and Corruption I," ch. 2.

7 See Aristotle, "Topics VIII," ch. 1.

8 See the excellent dialectical treatment of *Man* done recently by Mortimer Adler, *The Difference of Man and the Difference It Makes*, (New York: Holt, Rinehart and Winston Co., 1967); also read *The Phenomenon of Man*, which is well done dialectically by Pere T. de Chardin.

9 See Saint Thomas Aquinas, *In Boethium de Trinitate*, q. 6, a. 1, ad 1.

10 See also Aristotle, "Metaphysics I," chs. 6, 10.

11 See Saint Thomas Aquinas, *Contra Gentiles I*, chs. 2–14; also W. A. Wallace, *The Role of Demonstration in Moral Theology* (Wash., D.C.: The Thomist Press, 1962); also M. A. Glutz, *The Manner of Demonstrating in Natural Philosophy* (River Forest, Illinois: Aquinas Press, 1956).

12 This argument is an adaptation of the one that can be found in *An Anatomical Exercise on the Motion of the Heart and Blood in Animals* (1628) by William Harvey, M.D.; cf. the interpretation of Chapter 9 of this work by Dr. H. A. Ratner in *The Thomist*, vol. 24 (1961), pp. 175–208.

13 This argument is an adaptation. See Saint Thomas Aquinas, *Commentary on Posterior Analytics II*, ch. 8, lesson 7.

14 This argument is an adaptation. See T. de Chardin, S.J., *Le Milieu Divin*, p. 56.

15 (same as footnote 13)

16 See Aristotle, "Posterior Analytics I," ch. 2.